Airline Passenger Screening Has Become a FEMA-TYPE SNAFU

The Screening System Developed During 1969-70 Holds The Key To Refocusing On Modern Day Terrorism

David H. Brown

authorHOUSE™

1663 LIBERTY DRIVE, SUITE 200
BLOOMINGTON, INDIANA 47403
(800) 839-8640
WWW.AUTHORHOUSE.COM

AuthorHouse™
1663 Liberty Drive, Suite 200
Bloomington, IN 47403
www.authorhouse.com
Phone: 1-800-839-8640

AuthorHouse™ UK Ltd.
500 Avebury Boulevard
Central Milton Keynes, MK9 2BE
www.authorhouse.co.uk
Phone: 08001974150

First published by AuthorHouse 4/26/2006

ISBN: 1-4259-3762-4 (dj)
ISBN: 1-4259-0632-X (sc)

Library of Congress Control Number: 2005910586

Printed in the United States of America
Bloomington, Indiana

This book is printed on acid-free paper.

PROLOGUE

This updated sequel is a revision and expansion of my previous book on airline passenger screening titled, *NINE/ELEVEN.* In some instances, I have used literary license.

Airline passenger screening by the Transportation Security Administration (TSA) in particular, and Mideast terrorism in general, have elements in common. The government should relearn the basic meticulous approaches and conclusions from the original screening program.

I also submit that Mideast terrorists have outsmarted us by switching targets and tactics.

The following observations are based on my unique professional experience:

(1) Mideast terrorists have easier targets of opportunity in the U.S. with lower risk than to repeat the kamikaze-type attacks of 9/11/2001.

(2) Mideast terrorists are winning the psychological war. Just a rumor of an intended incident spreads fear in this country. And, their audience is as much Islam as U.S.

(3) Mideast terrorists have succeeded in diverting billions of U.S. dollars from our domestic needs. How long can we balance both requirements?

(4) The government continues to treat the symptoms of Mideast terrorism, not address the root causes.

TABLE OF CONTENTS

ABOUT THE AUTHOR

I began a 24-year federal career in 1967 as assistant director of information at the Department of Justice. I later transferred to the Federal Aviation Administration, then to the Department of Transportation, and in 1974 became the first professional public affairs officer at the Government Printing Office, retiring in 1991. In 1976, 1 founded and was first president of the National Association of Government Communicators. So, I understand government.

An Infantry rifleman in World-War II, I later began a 28-year career as an Army Reserve officer, retiring as a lieutenant colonel in 1978. For the final 12 years, I had a mobilization assignment with the Office of the Chief of Information in the Pentagon. I also graduated from the 4-year 2-week Advanced Infantry Course at Fort Benning, Georgia, where tactics were discussed at length. In addition, I attended a two-week seminar on Cold War Strategy at the Army Command and General Staff College at Fort Leavenworth, Kansas. Further, in 1959, I was part of a 15-member Joint Information Task Force to deal with reporters from all over the U.S. who covered the first post-World War II exercise to determine how successfully thousands of troops could be airlifted to Ramey Air Force Base in Puerto Rico, called Operation Big Slam/Puerto Pine. My World War II military decorations include the Meritorious Service Medal, Combat Infantry Badge, and Bronze Star Ribbon with battle star. So, I understand the military.

Starting as a copy boy at The Cleveland Press, I later worked at the Circleville Herald, became state editor of The Columbus Citizen, and returned to The Press, spanning nearly 15 years on Ohio newspapers. I developed and taught media relations courses at the Department of Agriculture Graduate School, and taught journalism courses at a community college. During two newspaper strikes, I worked at two local television stations. So, I understand the media

In 1967, I was the sole government spokesman at the Lorton, Virginia detention facility where the 600 Pentagon demonstrators were held for three days. During 1969-70, I was the spokesman for the Federal Aviation Administration's Task Force on Deterrence of Air Piracy that developed the original airline passenger screening system. In 1971, I was the government spokesman at Fort Dix, New Jersey at the press conference announcing training of armed sky marshals. So, I understand government, the military, and the news media.

There is a connection between present day *Mideast terrorist* hijacking of U.S. aircraft and the *non-terrorist* hijacking of U.S. aircraft more than three decades ago.

First, if you want to deal with hijackers, you have to think like hijackers. We accomplished that when Task Force member and then FAA chief psychologist Dr. John T. Dailey developed a list of some two dozen characteristics common to most hijackers into a behavioral profile that would help identify potential hijackers. I was on the team that tested the profile at nine airports, discovering that it fit no more than 2 percent of the flying public screened. We concluded such a small number of "suspects" would enable the system to quickly clear the other 98 percent. And, that should still be the basis for current screening procedures - quickly clear the innocent.

Second, if you want to deal with terrorists, you have to understand terrorism. In essence, terrorists are guerilla fighters. They are not necessarily clearly organized as our troops are. They seek political or even religious objectives, while we are concerned with military objectives. I fear that time is more on the side of Mideast terrorists than on ours.

Third, efforts to deal with terrorism must be flexible. This is evidenced in the variety of locations and types of tactics the terrorists use. Dr. Dailey always maintained that his profile of 1969-70 fit only those times.

The Task Force Final Report in 1978, which is FAA Manual AM-78-35, contained enough warnings about the possibility that terrorists might hijack U.S. aircraft so that 9/11 could have been prevented. Intelligence dysfunctions notwithstanding, all that our decision makers had to do was connect the dots between our predictions and terrorist activity such as the 1993 World Trade Center bombing that was highly publicized in the media.

David H. Brown

CHAPTER ONE - IF IT'S BROKE, FIX IT

Panic has given birth to the fraternal twins Department of Homeland Security and Transportation Security Administration. Their godfathers are Department of Transportation and Federal Aviation Administration, relatively speaking.

There is a saying on The National Archives wall in downtown Washington, D.C. copied from Shakespeare's "The Tempest." It reads: "The Past is Prologue." George Santayana, in his "The Life of Reason," wrote: "Those who cannot remember the past are condemned to repeat it."

And, that is exactly how to describe the Rube Goldberg approach to airport passenger screening that is in vogue today, and its relationship to Mideast terrorism.

The current screening system is not as efficient nor effective as it could be because it is based on a set of faulty premises and assumptions. The past needs to be re-examined for sensible repairs. Instead, decision makers are acting like hamsters, running fast in place and getting nowhere. On July 12, 2005, the Secretary of the Department of Homeland Security announced yet another "reorganization."

With the fifth anniversary of 9/11 coming up in 2006, just what has been accomplished? Mideast terrorists, and their disciples, keep changing their *modus operandi*, but we have not. We seem bent on remodeling the Edsel instead of redesigning a new vehicle to fight terrorism.

We seem to be trying to combat terrorism in the 21st century with 20th century tactics. For the first time, this country is fighting religious-based scattered guerillas, not an organized government-based. army. The demolition of organized Iraqi military forces was textbook tactics. But, instead of the end of the book, we find more and more unexpected chapters. We literally need a new beginning, and experience from the original airline passenger screening effort will help.

CHAPTER TWO - THE INTERVIEW BEGINS

S M: "Mr. Brown, I am a staff member of the National Commission on Terrorist Attacks Upon the United States, most often called the 9/11 Commission. I am telephoning you because it has come to our attention that you have written a book on airport security based on a Federal Aviation Administration Task Force that only was in effect for a year and a half."

DB: "Actually, I already have written one titled *NINE/ELEVEN*. I am working on a sequel titled, *MIDEAST TERRORISTS MAY NOT BOTHER WITH ANOTHER 9/11.*

SM: "That's very provocative. Can you come in for an interview?"

DB: "I would be happy to do so. Dr. John T. Dailey, my colleague, is a frail 89 years old, but I have his background material."

SM: "Thank you for coming. Where should we start?"

DB: "I would like to begin with what passes for airline passenger screening today, and why I feel it is not accomplishing the task for which it was developed more than three decades ago. Our Final Report, issued in 1978 as FAA Manual AM-78-35, described pre-Task Force efforts as a poorly coordinated rush toward prevention with assorted, often contradictory, determinations regarding useful means of control. How does that sound when compared to today's efforts?"

SM: "What do you mean by that?"

DB: "I brought along my first book because it is the only one that contains the behind-the-scenes look at how screening was first developed by that Task Force during 1969-70. Airlines knew our conclusions. One of those conclusions ironically predicted that 'mass hijacking of U.S. aircraft could also be carried out by an organized group in order to achieve terrorist objectives.'"

SM: "Are you implying the Task Force predicted 9/11 ?"

DB: "In a way, yes. But, we did not envision those hijacked aircraft would be used as flying missiles. However, all of the nine members of the team were well aware of how the Japanese used suicide attacks against our naval forces in the Pacific during World War II."

SM: "Then, what are you implying?"

DB: "I need to go back in time to the origin of the Task Force, and what our goal was before I connect it with the present. There are those who wonder why the effort was turned over to the Office of Aviation Medicine. The Final Report explained that the Task Force needed to be made up of specialists from many disciplines 'to explore all facets of (skyjacking) in a simultaneous, coordinated and systematic manner.' The field of medicine utilizes an approach called epidemiology which looks into the 'nature of a disease, to substantiate a conclusion statistically, to pinpoint locations of an outbreak and to define within reasonable levels of accuracy the elements of the outbreak and the probabilities for its continued spread.' Thus, this approach points up the similarities to be found in effective efforts to track down elusive disease-causing entities and control of the kinds of circumstances involved in air piracy - assuming, of course, that epidemiological methodology is appropriately modified and applied to (air piracy).'"

SM: "That is a mouthful and a half, but I think I understand this approach."

DB: "That set the tone for our group, chaired by Dr. H.L. (Rick) Reighard, the FAA's federal air surgeon. Our top priority clearly was to develop and test a system that could help stem the tide of aircraft hijackings, most of which went to Cuba. But, by the very title of the group, we knew early on that there never could be one system that could *eliminate* all hijackings."

SM: "So, what was your goal?"

DB: "Our goal was to try to reduce hijacking *attempts* to a manageable number. The odds of dealing with such problems are infinitely better on the ground than in the air."

SM: "How did you hope to do that?"

DB: "We did not have the luxury of any precedents to guide us. But, the luck of timing stepped in. Dr. Dailey had been working on creating psychological profiles for years. By the time he joined the FAA as chief psychologist in early 1968, he had developed and applied dozens of profile tests to several million Air Force and Navy personnel, as well as to students at Texas, Pittsburgh, and George Washington Universities. On February 6, 1969, Congressman Harley 0. Staggers chaired a hearing of his House Committee on Interstate and Foreign Commerce. Dr. Dailey's closed-door plea to test his new behavioral profile as Step One of a passenger screening system turned out to be the key for a Committee mandate ordering the FAA to create the Task Force."

SM: "I heard somewhere that the Task Force was disbanded after only a year and a half. Does that mean you accomplished your goal in such a short time?"

CHAPTER THREE - VITAL MISTAKES

DB: "Yes, but disbanding our Task Force was one of two horrific mistakes that changed the course of history. However, to respond to your statement, Dr. Reighard said from the beginning that he hoped our work would lead to the establishment of a permanent office within the FAA. He lobbied to have Task Force members form the nucleus of a permanent entity. Pages 76-80 of the Final Report contain recommendations for the staffing. But, when the Office of Air Transportation Security was created shortly after we were disbanded in August 1970, only our security representative joined it full time. Another member became sort of a consultant."

SM: "Why was that a mistake? Sounds more like bureaucratic sour grapes."

DB: "That broke the link between what we accomplished and what was implemented later on. The new Office personnel literally had to reinvent the wheel. We did the testing. On the one hand, the passengers we interviewed did not have any objections to some sort of search. I was on the testing team that went to all nine airports, and I videotaped passenger reaction. More important, Dr. Dailey concluded from the data the other members of the testing team garnered that no more than **2 percent** of the flying public fit enough of his profile to be subjected to a further and more intensive search and interrogation. We wanted a procedure that had verified merit, and that focused on the most **likely** potential hijackers. In doing so, we could facilitate screening out the other 98 percent of passengers. In my previous book, I pointed out that airlines warned that we would ruin air travel by *overly intrusive* searching. But, if we could quickly and efficiently clear those 98 percent, detaining the 2 percent would be manageable and tolerable."

SM: "Even with all the searching going on today, air travel is not suffering."

DB: "No, but the current procedure has not caught any Mideast terrorists. And, results are highly suspect, if you will forgive the pun. Look at what we have today. The media keep reporting cases of searches that humiliate many older and many younger passengers, of equipment that breaks down, of security personnel who are not doing a professional job, et cetera, et cetera, et cetera. On May 8, 2005, The New York Times had this headline: 'U.S. to Spend Billions More to Alter Security Systems.'"

SM: "You said there were two mistakes. What was the other one?"

DB: "That took place during what has been labeled 'Black September of 1970.' Following a sort of truce between Israel and Egypt, several radical organizations broke away from the Palestine Liberation Organization, or PLO. One, the Popular Front for the Liberation of Palestine, or PFLP, decided to hijack four airplanes to gain the release of fellow guerillas whom the Israelis had captured and who were sent to Swiss jails. On September 6, a Nicaraguan man and a Palestinian woman hijacked El Al Flight 219 that had taken off from Tel Aviv headed for New York's JFK Airport. El Al guards aboard the flight killed the man and captured the woman, Leila Khaled. The plane flew on to London's Heathrow Airport. On that same day, two hijackers, who were supposed to be on the El Al flight but who were bumped off because the plane was full, hijacked Pan Am Flight 93 after it left Brussels also headed for JFK. They flew to Beirut to refuel, and several other hijackers got aboard. The plane finally landed in Cairo, Egypt. After all passengers and crew left the plane, the hijackers blew it up. TWA Flight 74 was hijacked after it left Frankfurt Germany, and was flown to a former British Royal Air

Force base in Jordan called Dawson's Field. Swissair Flight 100 was hijacked after leaving Zurich, and also taken there."

SM: "That was some feat."

DB: "That wasn't all. Three days later, a lone hijacker took over BOAC Flight 775 and brought it to Dawson's Field. It turned out the hijacker was not a member of the PFLP, but a Palestinian sympathetic to the cause who wanted Khaled freed."

SM: "What happened then?"

DB: 'The hijackers cut a deal for the release of Khaled, after which they blew up the three planes at Dawson's Field."

SM: "You said 'Black September' was a mistake."

DB: "Shortly afterward, the Nixon administration ordered that all passengers boarding U.S. planes were to be searched."

SM: "So, what's wrong with that?"

DB: "What's wrong is that *not one* of those aircraft was hijacked in the United States. Why order the screening of all passengers in *our* country when the hijackings took place in *other* countries?"

SM: "I repeat, what's wrong with that?"

DB: "Actually, that very good question leads directly into formation of our Task Force. Other countries around the world have their own systems of screening passengers. We only developed and tested a viable procedure for screening passengers in the United States. While we looked at how other countries dealt with hijackers, we focused on what was feasible in our nation. We concluded that what works in one country does not necessarily work in other countries."

SM: "Let's back up a bit to where the Task Force came into being."

CHAPTER FOUR - BIRTH OF A CREATION

DB: "Little more than a week after the Staggers Committee mandate, FAA Acting Administrator Dave Thomas tepidly created the Task Force on Deterrence of Air Piracy. The term 'deterrence' is very important."

SM: "Why is that?"

DB: "Because, we agreed that there was no way we could eliminate all hijackings. Our goal was to get the odds in our favor by developing a procedure targeted for a manageable number of what we called 'suspects.' We felt from the beginning that trying to screen every airline passenger would be inefficient, ineffective, and disruptive."

SM: "But, aren't all passengers screened today? Are you implying that the current procedures are, to use your own words, inefficient, ineffective, and disruptive?"

DB: "For the most part, yes. But there are some good elements to the current system."

SM: "All right, continue with the Task Force time line."

DB: "Except for Dr. Reighard and Dr. Dailey, who as chief psychologist was on his staff, none of the team members knew each other. We came from diverse disciplines: Lowell L. Davis from Flight Standards Service; Joseph K. Blank from Office of Compliance and Security; Max Collins from Aircraft Development; John E. Marsh from Office of General Counsel; Robert K. Friedman from Office of Management Systems; E. Lee Jett from Office of International

Aviation Affairs, and me from Office of Public Affairs. Thus, we had input from specialists in security, operations, engineering, law, management, international aviation, behavioral sciences and medicine, and media relations. By the end of our work, as diverse professionally as we were, we had become friends and even socialized together."

SM: "Isn't that unusual for government workers?"

DB: "Yes. But, I like to feel we were the right persons together at the right time for the right purpose. That is not to say it started out that way. I only can speak for myself. As the press officer, I was treated with cool hostility. I had the distinct feeling the others felt that I would blab everything to the news media. Some of our work had to be secret. I actually had to be 'tested' by some of the group."

SM: "Go on."

DB: "Dr. Reighard seemed the wrong choice to be chairman. He was basically a very shy person. He told me once that he was not even comfortable holding a staff meeting with his own people. As a physician, he had a keen sense of diagnosing problems before prescribing remedies. In hindsight, I only now realize that his medical approach to hijacking was so right on target. *Because of that, I firmly believe Mideast terrorism is a cancer on society. If not treated properly, it will become more virulent and spread.* Getting back to Dr. Reighard, he listened to everyone, and encouraged all of us to exchange views and information. As a result, we effectively worked 'outside of the box.' We wanted results, and were willing to take chances with new approaches to what we found in our testing phase. We did not want to be tied down by bureaucratic red tape. We had to find a way to deter potential hijackers from boarding their flights in the first place. *Ironically, that is the same Number One priority today!*"

SM: "Well, if the Number One priority has not changed, why are you so critical of what is going on today?"

DB: "When we did our work, hijackers were not Mideast terrorists. They were for the most part ordinary citizens who wanted to hijack aircraft, but not to kill passengers or themselves. The 9/11 hijackers were suicide terrorists who wanted to kill both themselves and all the other passengers to make their political statement."

CHAPTER FIVE - THE **PROPER FOCUS**

SM: "That's an interesting distinction."

DB: "Dr. Dailey's behavioral profile was focused on screening out *potential* hijackers while facilitating the boarding of the other 98 percent of the passengers. So, the basic premise was that passengers were *innocent* until the profile, plus subsequent search and interrogation, proved otherwise. Today, all passengers are presumed to be potential Mideast terrorists until they can prove their innocense."

SM: "And, your point is?"

DB: "My point is that if all your security efforts are aimed at requiring 100 percent of the passengers to prove they are not potential Mideast terrorists, you just cannot have an efficient, effective, and non-humiliating search procedure. I say again, our goal was to efficiently and quickly facilitate the boarding of those 98 percent of passengers while focusing with those 2 percent suspects. The government should go back to Square One to determine how to identify potential Mideast terrorists. I emphasize *potential Mideast terrorists,* not Americans. Let me give you a personal example of how questionable the current system is."

SM: "This should be interesting."

DB: "Last year, my wife and I went on a tour of European countries. On our return, we had to change planes in Philadelphia for our flight back to Dulles International Airport. Of the 39 passengers, I was the only one selected for a personal search."

SM: "Why?"

DB: "I asked the same question. Believe it or not, the answer was, 'We have to search at least one person on every flight.'"

SM: "And, what was your response to this? Did you tell him you were on the team that developed passenger screening in the beginning?"

DB: "I tried a different tack. I offered my passport and my round-trip airline tickets. I tried to reason that a potential Mideast terrorist would not likely take his wife on a two-week European vacation before returning to the U.S. to do a dirty deed. One of the elements in our original profile was that hijackers would buy one-way tickets, not round-trip ones. 'Why spend the extra money when you are not going to be alive for the return flight?' I asked. He did not think that was funny. By the way, no one searched my wife."

SM: "If I understand what you are saying, it is that passengers with valid identification should not be searched the same way potential hijackers are. But, documents can be forged. That happened on 9/11."

DB: "There is a world of difference between searching for *potential Mideast terrorist hijackers* and searching for *potential non–Mideast terrorist hijackers.* By the way, I am a retired Army Reserve lieutenant colonel. I carry that photo-ID in my wallet. But, I will bet that still would not have satisfied that security guard.*"

SM: "Wait a minute. Didn't the 19 terrorists - I mean Mideast terrorists - have identification that passed security?"

DB: "Yes. And, that makes another point. Dr. Dailey's behavioral profile had some two dozen characteristics. Just one would not be cause for concern. If memory serves me correctly, at least half a dozen would be a minimum to label a passenger as a 'suspect.'"

SM: "What about the name-watch list that the FBI and CIA have developed?"

DB: "That's after-the-fact. Since there has been so much publicity about a name list, what terrorist in his right mind would continue to use a name that was likely to be on that list?"

SM: "I recall that in early July of 2005, a passenger was hauled off a flight because his name was on the name-watch list."

DB: "I am not denying that the name-watch list could have some value. In fact, there are numerous stories about planes that have made emergency landings, because after the flight was airborne authorities discovered a name on the list. Those stories also have pointed out that many innocent Mideast people have the same name. In 1976, way before all the terrorism took hold, I was stopped at JFK International Airport on a return trip from Israel, taken aside, and questioned. It seemed a New York City criminal with the same first, middle initial, and last name as mine was on the FBI's Most Wanted List. It took me several minutes to assure the officer that I never had resided in New York City."

SM: "Better safe than sorry, wouldn't you say?"

DB: "I would agree, only if you add sensible safe than sorry."

SM: " What's wrong with that? I remember that passenger who had an explosive device hidden in his shoe."

DB: "You are referring to the so-called 'shoe bomber.' He was a domestic nut case who professed a love for Mideast terrorism. As far as I can tell, *no terrorist hijacker born in the Middle East* has been found with such a device in his shoe on a U.S. airplane. Remember I pointed out that we could not eliminate all hijacking attempts. We readily admitted some attempts could breach any security system. As tight as security is in the Mideast, there still have been attempted terrorist activities while the aircraft was in flight."

SM: "So, are you saying the government should not check for another potential 'shoe bomber?'"

DB: "No. I am saying you have to identify what you are searching for, using a combination of the profile and technology. But, with proper ID, get the innocent passengers on board their flights.

SM: "Wow! I am confused."

DB: "What I am saying is that once the 'shoe bomber' incident was over, the metal detector screening system should have been adjusted to check for such a device. Merely triggering the magnetometer should not require a full body search if the passenger has proper ID, or can meet other clearance criteria."

SM: "Are you saying the detectors can be flexible?"

DB: "Each airline can adjust the detectors at various airports. Dr. Dailey always maintained that his behavioral profile was flexible enough to be adjusted depending on the type of hijackings taking place. A May 3, 2005 story in The New York Times noted that a female FBI agent was allowed to pass through security with her pistol, but her nail file was confiscated as a potential weapon."

SM: "We seem to be getting deeper and deeper into this, and I apologize for having to take another break. I have another commitment this afternoon. I wonder if you could return the day after tomorrow."

DB: "Absolutely."

CHAPTER SIX - THE PRE-BOARDING PROFILE

SM: "Let"s start off today with what steps can keep the hijackers from boarding."

DB: "We need to understand the behavioral approach. Citing the Final Report, this approach 'is statistical in character and involves analysis of such factors as: (1) What kinds of persons engage in a particular activity? (2) How do they go about it? (3) Why do they do it?"

SM: " Why is this important?"

DB: "Again, we turn to the Final Report: 'Examination of statistical probabilities tends to reveal when and under what circumstances the unwanted activity may take place.' The difference between what we did then, and what is going on now, is that there are no 'statistical probabilities' in current procedures. The government merely decided to screen everyone, as if that simple procedure would address the complex problem. And, that is why Dr. Dailey's profile gained so much credibility."

SM: "If I understand what you are saying, this methodical approach is what led to what you call success."

DB: "Yes, and I am glad you used the term 'success.' Let me put it another way. In 1961, Congress passed the Air Piracy Act. That made it a crime to try to hijack an airplane. I submit that is all well and fine for rational people like you and me. It certainly does not address terrorists, who are irrational by our definition. We must keep in mind that the 9/11 terrorist hijackers could not care less about the Air Piracy Act. They were going to die, and so were all the passengers. And, again keep in mind, our work was not concerned with Mideast terrorist hijackers. All I am saying is that before the current procedures were rushed into action, they should have been subjected to the same methodological approach we used."

SM: "All right, let's get back to the purpose of the profile once it was proposed."

DB: "I must reiterate that we never hoped to keep all **potential** hijackers from boarding. We wanted to deal with a manageable number."

SM: "I will try to remember that. How did you hope to accomplish that goal?"

DB: "That is where Dr. Dailey proved so invaluable. Using his previous profiling experience with the FAA's own two-stage screening program for civilian pilots, John conducted an exhaustive research of all previous hijackings - successful or not - to create the most complete data bank on the subject in existence. He and I also produced the first complete list of hijackings, which were used not only by the International Civil Aviation Organization, as well as by many countries throughout the world, and also by the various news media."

SM: "What did Dr. Dailey's research conclude?"

DB: "He discovered that a number of characteristics seemed to discriminate innocent passengers from past hijackers who posed as innocent passengers. He refined that list down to about two dozen characteristics that would avoid being labeled 'racial profiling.' Let me cite public data from Pages 58-59 of the Final Report: 'After evaluating what was learned during testing, Task Force members placed emphasis on accumulating data on the age and sex of passengers; place, time, and payment of tickets; boarding sequence; pre-boarding activity; time of day, origin of flight, type of aircraft, destination, duration of flight, segment traveled, and geographic direction of flight; whether the passenger traveled alone or was with someone; whether the passenger had carry-on luggage and had luggage checked in the boarding sequence; and, seat selection.' A one-way ticket was an obvious clue."

SM: "You've got to be kidding me. Those are just common sense."

DB: "Sometimes the obvious escapes you. But, John was meticulous. Anyhow, that became Step One in our proposed procedure.'

SM: "For the sake of argument, let's say someone triggered enough of that profile to make them suspect. What then?"

DB: "Step Two would require that person to produce valid identification. Step Three would require that person to pass through a metal detector called a magnetometer. That is the same off-the-shelf device soldiers used in World War II to locate land mines. It's the same device people use on beaches to find discarded worthwhile metal objects."

SM: "And, then?"

DB: "Step Four would involve a body scan by a hand-held version of the magnetometer, followed by extensive interrogation."

SM: "Do I infer from what you have described that it is important to conduct those steps in the order you have listed?"

DB: "Absolutely! We concluded that upsetting that procedure would render the system ineffective. In fact, that issue came up in a court case I will discuss later."

SM: "Now that you had this procedure, what did you do next?"

DB: "We needed to test John's profile."

SM:"Why?"

DB: "First, we needed to find out if it provided a viable approach. Second, we needed to know how many passengers fit enough of that profile to be set aside."

CHAPTER SEVEN -
TESTING, TESTING - STEP ONE

SM: "How were you going to conduct the testing?"

DB: "At first, the group wanted to try it out only at New York's LaGuardia Airport and Miami's International Airport. Those seemed to be the favorite boarding places. Then, someone wanted to include Washington's National Airport."

SM: "Sounds reasonable."

DB: "I was the newest and youngest member of the Task Force, but my gut feeling was that we needed more testing sites. Early in my newspaper career, I had done some market research, and it taught me to get enough inclusion in the research so that the results would not get skewed."

SM: "Screwed?"

DB: "No, s-k-e-w-e-d. I did not want the results to be distorted."

SM: "How did the others react?"

DB: "Bless Dr. Reighard, he agreed immediately. He relied on his medical background to get as much unbiased data as possible before reaching a conclusion. We finally agreed on five other airports around the country, and the airport in San Juan, Puerto Rico."

SM: "What was your reasoning?"

DB: "I felt passengers flew in and out of different parts of the country for different reasons."

SM: "How did the others react to that?"

DB: "Well, not as bad as they did to my next suggestion."

SM: "And, what was that one?"

DB: "To be honest, I sucked in my breath, and then recommended that we hold press conferences at every one of the airports. I got some angry stares, believe me. But first, I have to explain how we were going to conduct the tests, and how the press conference would fit in."

SM: "Go ahead."

DB: 'Dr. Reighard determined that the testing team would consist of Lowell Davis, Max Collins, and me. Lowell had been a Navy pilot; Max had been a civilian one. Our work would be only with Eastern Air Lines at its gates at each one of the airports."

SM: "Why Eastern?"

DB: "At the time, it was the most hijacked airline."

SM: "Sounds reasonable."

DB: "There would be two parts to the testing. As I pointed out before, one was to determine what percentage of Eastern's passengers fit enough of the profile to be labeled a 'suspect.' The second was for me to use a videotape recorder to document passenger reaction. Actually, there really was a third, now that I think of it. Since I got the go-ahead to hold press conferences, that would give us a clue to media reaction."

SM: "What was your routine?'

DB: "First, we visited the designated airport. We checked out the test gate, and Lowell and Max briefed gate personnel. Then, about two weeks later, we flew back to set up the magnetometer and my videotape recorder. Also, I had alerted the news media in that city that a press conference would be held to test a passenger screening system designed to discourage potential hijackers. Thanks to Lowell and Max, the testing went smoothly. As passengers passed through our portable magnetometer, Eastern personnel would ask passengers at random how they felt about being screened, while I videotaped their comments. Meanwhile, Lowell and Max would monitor Eastern gate personnel who had been briefed on the profile to keep track of how many passengers triggered it."

SM: "What about the reporters?"

DB: "We did our homework back in Dr. Reighard's office. My reasoning, based on nearly 15 years as an Ohio newspaper reporter before I became a government public information officer, was that the media would soon learn about the screening, and smell a story on why it was secret. I argued that if we told the media in advance about the magnetometer, we could nip in the bud any stories about how reporters 'beat a secret system.' In fact, we invited the reporters to go through the detector. I also tried to anticipate questions the reporters would ask, and the rest of the team helped me formulate the proper answers."

SM: "What if the reporters asked questions about the profile?"

DB: "Thanks to the team, we worked out our response. All I would say was that we were developing a procedure that could identify potential hijackers that included electronic search. I would add that I could not reveal further details because of security concerns."

SM: "How did that work out?"

DB: "Of course, reporters wanted to know all about that profile. When I would not give specifics, they usually pressed me hard for details. Oh, sorry for that pun."

SM: "How did you handle that?"

DB: "The response probably would not work today, what with such a determined news media. I would say that if I revealed the details, any potential hijacker would know how to beat the profile. I would ask, 'If you revealed the profile, would you want a member of your family, or even yourself, to be on the next flight out?' As expected, there were those few reporters who scoffed at the testing. What helped was that, with the team's agreement, I would announce that this was an experimental system that was not foolproof, but was an approach we felt would help find the way to deal with the hijackings."

SM: "How did the reporters react to that?"

DB: "We had established a good rapport with the news media with our press conferences. As the Final Reported noted, 'The Task Force took particular care to offer the same advantage to each press representative and to supply the same story no matter which media were served.' A few reporters complained that I had destroyed their 'scoop' about how they beat a full-proof system. One reporter even said to me, 'This is the first time I ever heard a press officer admit the govemment had a system that was not perfect.' Of some 200 stories, only six were negative."

SM: "Sounds like a very smooth operation."

DB: "Actually, we almost never got off the ground, so to speak. Lowell was suspicious of me from the start because he had experienced some run-ins with reporters while he was in the Navy. He said out loud that I probably would blab everything to reporters. However, after our first trip, he saw the positive media reaction, and we became close friends after that. I honestly do not recall whose idea it was, but I was given a black-and-white videotape recorder and told to film passenger reaction. That turned the corner for an eventual all-gate all-airline test at New Orleans in mid-1970."

SM: "How long after your initial visit would you set up your test?"

DB: "Usually a couple of weeks. We would start at 7 am. to set up the equipment and get things in order for the day's flights. I usually held a press conference in mid-afternoon so the television stations would have stories for the evening news programs. Around 7 p.m., we would pack up and return to our hotel to discuss what we had learned. We found varying reasons airline passengers took trips to and from different locations. That helped Dr. Dailey tailor his behavioral characteristics depending on the airport. Some airport terminals had different configurations, so the magnetometer locations in the security areas would have to be flexible.'"

SM: "Anything else you learned?

DB: "Oh, yes. The Task Force arranged to produce airport signs warning of searches. I contacted the Voice of America to provide us with a Spanish translation. One day, I received a call from a San Diego airport official who pointed out that the Spanish translation we had provided was not the Spanish spoken in that area. So, we had to have two different translations."

SM: "That must have been embarrassing."

DB: "Well, it was unexpected. But then, so was the revelation that the Department of Agriculture maintained an inspection station at the San Juan airport that could double as our screening agent. We also discovered that Customs Bureau agents also operated at other airports, and they too could act as passenger screeners."

SM: "And, you followed the same routine at all the airports?"

DB: "Yes. After each one, Dr. Reighard gathered the Task Force members for a full-blown exchange of information and conclusions."

SM: "And, what were the conclusions?"

DB: "Perhaps the most startling one came when Dr. Dailey analyzed the data we had collected and concluded that no more than 2 percent of Eastern passengers fit-enough of the profile at most airports, and as low as 5-tenths of 1 percent at the others."

SM: "What was the significance of that?"

DB: "It told us that if we could concentrate on no more than 2 percent of the flying public, we had a chance of realistically coping with aircraft hijackings. No, we were not ignoring the other passengers. As I said before, we wanted the other 98 percent cleared for boarding as efficiently as possible. And, we wanted a pre-boarding procedure that had the best chance for success."

CHAPTER EIGHT - THE OPPOSITION

SM: "Did the team feel the airlines would buy your concept?"

DB: "The obvious question was whether our data would be the same with airlines other than Eastern. The only way to do that was to pick a new airport and involve every airline there."

SM: "And, that airport was . .

DB: "New Orleans."

SM: "How were you going to get the other airlines to go along with that?"

DB: "The senior vice presidents of all the airlines servicing New Orleans were called into a meeting in the FAA's administrator's 9th floor conference room. When our team entered the room, those executives were seated around the oval-shaped table glaring at us. Mike Fenello, Eastern's senior vice president and literally our 'god father,' called the meeting to order. But, before he could go on, one of the other senior vice presidents stood up and said he had a statement to make on behalf of his colleagues."

SM: "Did you feel that was good news or bad news?"

DB: "Bad."

SM: "What did that executive say?"

DB: "He announced that the airlines had commissioned the Menninger Institute, that internationally known psychiatric center in Minnesota, to evaluate what we were doing."

SM: "And?""

DB: "He said the Menninger empirical analysis 'supported our conclusion that your system will put us out of business because passengers will be afraid to go through the search process before they board their flights.'"

SM: "What was the Task Force reaction to that?"

DB: "Fenello called on Dr. Reighard and Dr. Dailey to detail the results of our work. When that did not seem to sway the airline executives, Fenello disclosed that I had videotaped all the tests, and without exception, passengers were willing to be searched because at least the government was trying to do something positive, especially a United Nations diplomat. When Fenello asked if they would like to see the tapes, along with a stack of news stories lauding our testing, you could have heard a feather hit the floor. Then, he said he would take that to mean there not any objection to having us equip all airlines at New Orleans as a final test. There was unanimous agreement"

SM: "Sounds brave, but weren't you literally putting all your eggs in one basket?"

DB: "Absolutely. But, Dr. Reighard said he had full confidence in Dr. Dailey's profile, and was satisfied that our testing had produced a viable procedure if the profile were Step One. When word got back to some of our superiors, they complained that we could be endangering the reputation of the FAA. We felt the risk was not as great as feared, based on the passengers' reaction. Also, the media were supportive, even though there were those stories speculating on how the procedure could be breached."

SM: "And, could it be breached?"

DB: "Of course. We maintained all along no system is perfect. When I was a cub reporter in a small Ohio town, I mentioned to a police sergeant that I was flabbergasted at hearing that a robber tried to hold up a bank in another city despite an armed guard and a security camera in the lobby. The sergeant told me the robber did not expect to be caught. I could not believe his answer. He replied that I did not think like a criminal, that I was too logical. *That is exactly what I think is wrong today. We do not think like Mideast terrorists. We continue to be 'surprised' when those terrorists change their tactics.*"

SM: "Don't tell me that all the publicity stopped hijacking attempts?"

DB: "The publicity was part of a psychological approach Dr. Dailey carefully crafted. He said putting obstacles in the way often deters criminals. And, hijackings stopped during our publicized testing period."

SM: "Any other effect the publicity had?"

DB: " It had one almost comical side effect we had not considered. It turned out that the profile also fit drug dealers, law breakers, illegal aliens, and so forth. I had a call from an Eastern Airline gate manager at LaGuardia who complained that his crews were discovering discarded weapons and drugs in potted plants near the gates. He even said, in a low voice, that since Mafia members flew Eastern to Florida, our work would discourage them. We did hear that drug dealers became convinced that the profile was only aimed at them."

SM: "You have got to be kidding me!"

DB: "Truth be told, that is what happened."

SM: "Any other unexpected side effects of the testing?"

DB: "One internal one. In return for Dr. Reighard's support for my openness with the news media, I said I would ask the team for help in formulating answers to reporters' technical questions. Also, I offered to coach any Task Force member so he could speak accurately to a reporter without having to clear with me because we all would provide the same answers. However, my superior went ballistic when I told him about my approach, and he insisted that all media calls would have to go through him. He never asked me to brief him, however."

SM: "'Let's get back to the final test at New Orleans."

CHAPTER NINE -
ALL OUR EGGS ARE IN ONE BASKET

DB: "Lowell, Max, and I did our usual trial run at New Orleans, and the others on our team coordinated with the airlines. With Dr. Reighard's approval, I contacted the local and national electronic and print media about the test. That was July of 1970. The airlines would choose the spokesman for a Thursday press conference."

SM: "Weren't you going to conduct it as you had done in the past?"

DB: "'Oh, no. Now, it was an airline show. I just coordinated the press alert. The news media were free to observe all the gates in operation and interview any passengers."

SM: "How did things go?"

DB: "Not as smooth as I thought they would. I had planned to fly down to New Orleans on that Monday with Lowell and Max. Dr. Dailey was to join us later. I had notified the media that I would be there on Monday. The Friday before, my superior called me into his office and said I could not leave until Tuesday, and that I had to be back in the office on Friday. Lowell, Max, and I had planned to take official leave on Friday and fly our wives down for a relaxing weekend."

SM: "What's that line about 'best laid plans' . . .?"

DB: "That's a line from a Robert Bums' poem... 'the best laid plans of mice and men oft go awry.' Anyhow, the only telephone call

I received all day was from an angry Ike Papas, correspondent for the Walter Cronkite television news show on CBS. He demanded to know why I wasn't in New Orleans to brief him. I gave him a lame excuse and said I would meet with him on Tuesday. He warned me that 'you had better be here, or my Thursday piece won't be one you like.'"

SM: "How did you handle that?"

DB: " I located Lowell and asked him to literally hold Ike's hand and give him as much as we could short of security. After all, a bad report on a major television news program would sink us so deep we never would recover."

SM: "So, you missed the press conference?"

DB: "Not only the press conference, but also the evening television news shows. Just before the press conference was to begin, I bumped into what seemed to be a still grumpy Papas. He told me he would wrap up his report right where I was standing, but he did not want me anywhere in sight. I was about to head back to the hotel and pack up when the correspondent for the Huntley-Brinkley news show on NBC saw me and apologized for getting to New Orleans only the day before. I said I was sorry for not being able to brief him, but he replied he got what he needed, and would stay for the press conference. So, here were two major television news shows that I felt I had shortchanged."

SM: "I get the impression you saw your career flashing before your eyes."

DB: "Did I ever. At the time both tv news programs were airing, I was on the plane headed home. I had called my wife earlier and asked her to watch both news shows. When I arrived around 8 p.m., she asked me if I was considering a career move. I stopped dead in my tracks, until she smiled and said we got glowing reports on both programs, especially Ike's report."

SM: "What happened when you got to the office the next day?"

DB: "My superior never said a word. I spent the day doing my travel report. The only telephone call I received came as I was about to go home for the day. It was from a top aide to Department of Transportation Secretary John A. Volpe, whom I also had alerted.

He said sternly that Mr. Volpe wanted to see the Task Force in his office the following Tuesday morning."

SM: "I guess you were somewhat apprehensive?"

DB: "That's an understatement. I was scared stiff. I asked the caller for a clue for the meeting. He paused long enough for me to sweat, then said that the Secretary had watched both programs and wanted to know how we got such good coverage for a project he never had been briefed about. He gave us a full hour, and was very complimentary."

SM: "Mr. Brown, I'm sorry but I have another appointment shortly. You really seem to have information we have not been able to find elsewhere. Can we resume this tomorrow at the same time?"

DB: "I'm more than happy to do it. And, thank you for asking me back."

CHAPTER TEN - DIRE PREDICTIONS

SM: "Thanks for continuing our dialogue despite interruptions. Where did we leave off.?"

DB: "We had briefed Secretary Volpe."

SM: "Oh, yes. What happened after that?"

DB: "Essentially, our work was done. But, before the Task Force was disbanded, we all sat down in Dr. Reighard's conference room and began to formulate some conclusions."

SM: "What were they?"

DB: "We discussed whether potential hijackers would continue to be deterred by our maximum publicity stating that various search procedures were going to be in place. As I mentioned before, we all agreed that an individual terrorist, or a group of terrorists, would try to find ways to defeat any pre-boarding procedure. We believed that determined terrorists would even try to shoot their way onto an airplane if they had to."

SM: "Was that addressed in your Final Report?"

DB: "Well, the Report contains three prophetic warnings about the future. For example, Page 39 states: 'There are too many people in too many parts of the world with motivations for violence to argue against expectations that (airplane hijackings) would not only spread but become differentiated in character.' On Page 88, you can find this observation: ' . . . as times, people, motivations, and methods of operation change, a continuing research ... would be needed to meet challenges already on the horizon.' But, Page 93 has what I feel is the definitive prediction: 'The Task Force was aware that mass hijacking of U.S. aircraft could also be carried out by an organized group in order to achieve terrorist activities.' Keep in mind these preceded 9/11 by 23 years. But, there was one more aspect."

SM: "What was that?"

DB: "Let me quote from Page 72 of our Final Report: 'Analysis of intelligence data available suggested that both the FAA and the air carrier industry would be well advised to prepare for possible future all out attacks on American air carrier transportation.'"

SM: "The Commission seems to conclude that intelligence gathering was dysfunctional."

DB: "Be that as it may, all I can point out is that quote came in our 1978 Final Report. That is why I made the statement that disbanding the Task Force in 1970 destroyed a vital link between then and now."

CHAPTER ELEVEN - SKY MARSHALS

SM: "Let me go back a bit to something you said earlier. So far, we have been talking about pre-boarding procedures. What about dealing with a hijacker, or hijackers, once the plane is in the air?"

DB: "One of the first things we did was to look carefully at how Israelis dealt with hijackers in the air. Our conclusion was that the United States was not prepared to take the same steps as found in El Al Airlines incidents. That is, armed guards were not afraid to shoot, even if it meant civilian casualties."

SM: "How else can you deal with this situation?"

DB: "We reasoned that we also would have to look at other onboard procedures in the event a terrorist, or group of them, got by the pre-boarding screening system. Using armed guards was one option. That brings me to the sky marshal alternative."

SM: "I had heard that airlines do use armed guards dressed as ordinary passengers."

DB: "Actually, the first effort in those says was to train military personnel to perform that task. In fact, I was assigned to be the spokesman for the first 'graduates' at a Fort Dix, New Jersey press conference."

SM: "Why you?"

DB: "It was a combination of my work with the Task Force, and my being an Army Reserve public information officer. As such, I was able to work closely with the military to carefully formulate what we would tell the media."

SM: "How did that work out?"

DB: "As is my lot, things began well, and then sank like a lead balloon."

SM: "What do you mean by that?"

DB: "I was in the middle of my presentation when I noticed a high-ranking Department of Transportation official walking up to the podium. He was not supposed to be part of the conference, but I had briefed him several weeks before because one of his responsibilities now that the Task Force was disbanded was to oversee the hijacking deterrence program. Obviously, he wanted to take over the press conference, so I did not have any choice but to introduce him."

SM: "How did that go?"

DB: "At first, it went well. He was saying the same words I had used in his briefing. Then, all of a sudden, he turned to me and asked whether we had any newly trained sky marshals on hand. I had to nod yes. He then ordered me to point them out. Well, doing that compromised these two men because their photos were all over the newspapers and on television. But, again, I did not have any choice. If that were not enough, he began talking about the weapons they would use. We did not want to reveal the special ammunition had been developed that would not damage the interior of any aircraft. He then ordered the two men to display those bullets. I was trying to back away when he told me to conclude the press conference, and walked away beaming. My military counterpart came over, patted me on the shoulder, and said he knew this was not my doing, that certainly I had been caught off guard. But I will admit to this. I caught up with the official and told him in no certain terms that he had destroyed a carefully planned news conference, had compromised two potential sky marshals, and had discussed a topic we wanted to avoid - the prospect of gun play at 35,000 feet in the air."

SM: "And, what was his reaction before he fired you?"

DB: "Would you believe he apologized to me? But, when I got back to my office, and after my superiors had seen the newspaper and television reports, there was no witness to his apology. I had to take the rap, but no, I did not get fired."

SM: "Tell me more about the sky marshal program"

DB: "After the Office of Air Transportation Security replaced our Task Force, an interim force of 800 soldiers was augmented by some 500 agents from the Bureau of Customs, the Secret Service, and the FBI were trained as sky marshals. Personnel from such Federal agencies as the National Park Service, the Fish and Wildlife Service, and the Postal Services also were trained under the Bureau. At one point, there were as many as 1,200 sky marshals traveling on random flights. But, as the years rolled on, the use of sky marshals diminished. Then, in 1985, Congress passed the International Security and Development Cooperation Act which validated the Federal Air Marshal program. In the interest of security, the FAA would not say how many sky marshals were in use, nor who they were. Nor would the agency reveal which flights they were on, or how they were trained."

SM: "That seems to follow along the approach you used with the media."

DB: "It was. But, here is a tidbit I got online from what was called The Marshals Monitor, the official site for the U.S. Marshals Service, part of the Department of Justice. There was one very interesting sentence that bears notice."

SM: "And, what was that?"

DB: "The sentence read: 'Legal guidelines stated that in order to perform a weapon search, there must be the solid belief that the person being searched could cause harm with the weapon and could cause a genuine fear for safety.' That was based on the Terry v Ohio case, which I would like to save for another time because it requires a lot of detail."

SM: "Okay. Let's continue with the sky marshal issue."

DB: "On January 14, 2002, the Los Angeles Times ran a story reporting that the sky marshal force has shrunk to 32 from a high of about 2,000 prior to 9/11. The story also stated that the force now had a goal of at least 2,000 sky marshals. It also asserted that on 9/11, sky marshals 'were in the wrong places - assigned to selected high-risk international flights, not domestic flights like the transcontinental routes targeted by Al Qaeda.' If that were not bad enough, the story quoted Douglas Laird, formerly head of security at Northwest Airlines, as claiming, 'What the government is doing is promoting a program to make people feel good.' To its credit, the story balanced this with a quote from O.K. Steele, former head of the FAA's security office, who asserted: ' . . . (the sky marshal program) has a deterrent effect."

SM: "Sounds like there certainly was turbulence in the program."

DB: "On August 10, 2003, The Miami Herald had an article reporting that some minority sky marshals claimed they were subjected to unfair treatment, including harassment."

SM: "I'm almost afraid to ask if there were any other problems."

DB: "MSNBC reported in July 2003 that the TSA was pulling sky marshals from some crosscountry and international flights 'because of budget problems associated with the costs of overnight lodging' for them."

SM: "What else could go wrong?"

DB: "You mean other than there not being an instance of sky marshals nabbing any Mideast terrorist hijackers? In 2003, the FAA issued a warning that several private firms in the West were illegally offering sky marshal training courses. The warning noted that sky marshals must be FAA employees. The warning added that some of the 'graduates' were issued a phony sky marshal badge, but had to buy their own weapons. The FAA never hired any of them."

SM: "I hope you do not have any more problem stories to relate."

DB: " Other than the complaints from many sky marshals about the boredom of cross-country and transoceanic flights, there is the fact that unfortunately the sky marshal program has a history of turbulence all along the way."

SM: "Again with the puns. But, okay, explain what you mean."

DB: "After the Department of Homeland Security was created after 9/11, one of its agencies was the Transportation Security Administration, which consolidated the government-wide airport security responsibility. The FAA's Office of Civil Aviation Security, as it was now called, was one of those folded into the TSA. On June 19, 2002, The Washington Post ran a story stating that members of the Federal Air Marshal Service, the sky marshals if you will, wanted to leave the TSA and join the new Bureau of Immigration and Customs Enforcement, although both were under TSA. They felt, according to the story, that they did not want to be in the same group as security officers who only worked at pre-boarding gates. Perhaps also contributing to this strife was a USA Today story a year earlier that claimed sky marshal applicants received curtailed training."

SM: "In reading your book, I was intrigued with your meeting with J. Edgar Hoover of the FBI that relates to security jurisdiction."

DB: "I had been transferred to the parent Department of Transportation News Division when I learned that there would be a press conference in Attorney General John Mitchell's office clarifying the responsibility of dealing with hijackers when a plane was still on the ground. The FBI would have the jurisdiction on the ground; the Department of Transportation would have the responsibility once the plane was in the air."

SM: "Where does Hoover come into all of this?"

DB: "I was talking with some of the reporters I had known when I worked for Attorney General Ramsey Clark when out of the corner of my eye I saw Hoover enter the room through a rear door. I expected to see his close aide, Clyde Tolson, with him. Then, I remembered that Tolson was on sick leave, part of a long illness. I must admit I thought this is a moment I cannot lose, so I walked over to Hoover who stood there alone. I introduced myself, explaining I had worked with my FBI counterpart Tom Bishop. Hoover lied when he said he remembered me now. But, here I was, chatting it up with Hoover, one on one, the rarest of opportunities. I never heard anyone having that opportunity ever."

SM: "Okay, you've got my attention now. What then?"

DB: "I asked Hoover if he had met the high-ranking Department of Transportation official who would be taking part in the press conference with him. He said no. I responded that I knew the official and would be happy to introduce Hoover to him. So, we walked over to the middle of the room where the official was standing. The talking stopped immediately when the reporters saw Hoover."

SM: "Is there some point to this?"

DB: "After I introduced the two, I backed off. A short time later, Ron Ostrow, the Los Angeles Times reporter who had covered the Justice Department when I worked there, rushed over to me and said, 'You S.O.B., why didn't you tell me you had an in with Hoover? I've been tying to interview him for eight years.'"

SM: "What was your response to that?"

DB: "I said, 'Ron, why didn't you ask me?' Truthfully, that was my first and only encounter with the infamous FBI director. That Department of Transportation official was the same one who ruined that sky marshal press conference at Fort Dix."

SM: "Let's get back to the sky marshals. How did the Task Force feel about armed officers on flights?"

DB: "Dr. Dailey and I were in the minority that felt this was not a feasible alternative."

SM: "Why not? It seems to have worked for the Israelis."

DB: "First of all, El Al has infinitely fewer flights than all U.S. airlines. Second, checking out potential terrorist hijackers in the Mideast was much simpler. And, third, the Mideast always seems to be on military alert. As I said before, we felt this was not an acceptable alternative for U.S. flights."

SM: "Any other reasons for your minority opinion?"

DB: " Dr. Dailey and I tried to point out that with some 30,000 flights a day throughout the U.S., it would take an army of marshals to protect each and every flight. Those guards would be subject to the same number of flying hours as flight crews, also meaning putting up with long times away from families. And, who would pay for all the increased costs that would result?"

SM: "But, I got the impression you had other approaches to in-flight measures."

CHAPTER TWELVE -
AIRBORNE PROTECTION

DB: "There was a cockpit device that was 100 percent lethal. We only saw a highly classified film of it, and we were horrified. Had that device been installed on the hijacked airplanes on 9/11, the terrorists would have died, allowing the U.S. cockpit crews to regain control of their aircraft."

SM: "Can you tell me more about that?"

DB: "No, I am afraid I can't. We were literally sworn to secrecy, and to my knowledge, it still is secret to this day."

SM: "But, if this device, whatever it was, was so good, why didn't the airlines install it?"

DB: "They were briefed on it, but for whatever reason, none decided to use it. Besides, the number of hijackings greatly diminished, so I would assume the airlines felt let well enough alone. But, one of the things we did accomplish, that had not been on our agenda, was the work of Lowell Davis."

SM: "What was that?"

DB: "You won't believe how simple it really was. Lowell always had been safety minded. He was the one who got the airlines to paint outlines of the exterior aircraft doors. He realized that during crashes, rescuers had a difficult time finding the exit doors. Even more than that, he was the one who insisted early on that cockpit doors needed to be more secure. Not only were too many doors flimsy, but they often were left open during some takeoffs."

SM: "That seems almost too simple."

DB: "Maybe so, but the cockpit door change has done more to protect the cockpit crew than almost anything else."

SM: "But, didn't the 9/11 terrorists get into the cockpits?"

DB: "Obviously, those cockpit doors could be breached at that time. To repeat, determined terrorists will use any means to accomplish their mission."

SM: "Well, if you have armed guards on board, they should be able to deal with in-flight problems."

DB: "Would you be surprised to learn that a year after our group was disbanded that a hijacker forced an American Airlines B-747 to Havana despite the fact that three air marshals and an FBI agent were on board?"

SM: "What about arming the cockpit crew?"

CHAPTER THIRTEEN - ARMING PILOTS

DB: "That is another issue where Dr. Dailey and I occupy the minority seat. Most aircraft cockpits are not 5-star hotel room size. They are crammed with instruments. Besides, while the plane is in the air, the captain and copilot are strapped into their seats. Let's say a hijacker got entry into the cockpit. Let's say the plane is on autopilot. Even if the left-seat captain can reach his shoulder holster, how is he or she going to be able to turn around enough to get a clear shot at the intruder? And, even if the right-seat copilot can draw his or her weapon, how is he or she going to be able to turn around enough to get a clear shot at the intruder? The fact is that the majority of pilots do not want to carry weapons because the chances of them being able to use their weapons effectively are not in their favor."

SM: "What about the hijacked flight that crashed in Pennsylvania?"

DB: "That effort by passengers to try to overpower the terrorists was courage rare in history. Everyone was going to die anyhow. But, to me, that validates our efforts to focus on keeping those people off the aircraft in the first place. And, I will not stop from emphasizing how important Dr. Dailey's profile is in identifying potential Mideast terrorists before they board."

SM: "How did you and Dr. Dailey feel about being in the minority?"

DB: "There continues to be much controversy over this subject. Let me start with the Department of Homeland Security first. On June 4, 2002, the Government Executive Magazine reported that TSA Director John Magaw told the Senate Commerce Committee: 'It's clear in my mind, when I weigh all of the pros and cons, pilots should not have firearms in the cockpit. If something does happen on that plane, they really need to be in control of that aircraft.' Yet, the same story noted that because there were not enough sky marshals to ride every flight, 'many members of Congress believe that armed pilots are a much better line of defense.'"

SM: "Sounds convincing."

DB: "The TSA and the Air Line Pilots Association agree with arming pilots. The article noted that ALPA points out armed pilots can defend the cockpit from inside, while sky marshals cannot. But, on the other hand, the Department of Transportation is against arming the cockpit crew, as are many pilots. Yet, a Los Angeles Times story in June 1972 stated that 'some captains believe that a gun at the head of the pilot is the greatest risk aloft.' On the other hand, the same story noted that other pilots claim 'a threat to a stewardess would be quite as effective as a gunman in the cockpit.'"

SM: "It just occurred to me that there might be a situation where the pilot is armed and there also are armed sky marshals on board."

DB: "I guess that is like an airborne version of the 1957 movie 'Gunfight at the OK Corral.' I don't mean to be flip about this, but yes, that could be a possibility. Anything could be possible. It is my understanding that the captain always is informed if an armed officer is on board. Again, this continues to support the Task Force conclusion that the greatest effort should be focused on keeping Mideast terrorists off the flight in the first place. By the way, a congressional report in 2003 revealed that two terrorists sneaked past security at a New York airport as a videotaped dry run well before 9/11. On 9/11, they sneaked box cutters aboard their flights."

SM: "What about other countries around the world? What is their view of arming pilots?"

DB: "The operative word seems to be caution. Of course, Israel has done it for years, in addition to uniformed guards. The BBC reported that England's Virgin Airlines preferred 'strengthening and protecting the security of the flight deck (read that to mean the cockpit door) and enhancing the screening and profiling of passengers and baggage.'"

SM: "Do I understand that pilots and crews are asked to report suspicious behavior?"

DB: "I came across that in a USA Today story in January 2004. The problem is that there does not seem to be an international data base to sift through all such information to give pilots an accurate warning of danger. And, there always is the danger that 'suspicious' actions can trigger unwarranted security action."

SM: "Didn't your book cite an example of that?"

DB: " You're referring to the Delta Flight 442 incident out of Atlanta in 2002. I use as my reference a story in the September 19, 2002 edition of The Philadelphia Inquirer. Two sky marshals were on board the flight to Philadelphia when a passenger was seen going through other people's luggage in the overhead bins. Their dealings with him led to another incident. Then, things got complicated. The marshals handcuffed the unruly man, rushed him to first-class, and pushed him into aisle Seat 1-C. The passenger in window Seat 1-D, a man of Indian descent but dressed in typical American clothing, had been reading a book. When he noticed what was happening, he stood up and asked to be moved. When one marshal sat down in 1-D to guard the unruly man, a flight attendant seated the passenger where the marshal had been. Meanwhile, back in the coach class, a woman wanted to switch seats with another woman on the aisle. For some reason, the second marshal must have thought this somehow was related to the handcuffed passenger. The marshal suddenly appeared at the partition dividing first-class from the coach section and, according to eye witnesses, he drew his pistol and ordered: 'Nobody move, nobody look down the aisle, nobody takes pictures or you will go to jail, nobody do anything.'"

SM: "Like I said, this sounds like a television movie."

DB: "One eye witness was Philadelphia Common Please Court Judge James Lineberger."

SM: "Now, that's an eye witness."

DB: "About half an hour later, the plane landed in Philadelphia. No sooner had the cabin door opened when local police officers came aboard to help the one marshal take the handcuffed prison off the plane. Finally, the passengers began to stand up, expecting to get off the plane. Before anyone could disembark, the second marshal went over to where the Indian man was sitting in first-class and ordered, 'Head down, hands over your head!' He was handcuffed and whisked off to the airport police station. Ironically, the woman who had been involved in the incident in coach was the Indian man's wife. She could not get a seat in first-class, so the couple had to be separated."

SM: "Are you sure this is not a television movie?"

DB: "Things got worse in a hurry. The Indian man was placed into a cell he later described as so filthy 'I wouldn't even put my dog in it.' The officers demanded his name, address, and Social Security number. When he asked why he was being treated that way, he said one responded, 'We didn't like the way you looked at us.' He later would say he never looked up at either sky marshal. After three hours, he was told to leave. No explanation. He and his wife finally were reunited."

SM: "Who was this Indian man?"

DB: "His name was Dr. Robert Rajcoomar, a naturalized U.S. citizen since 1985. He had been a medical major in the Army, and currently had been in private practice for nearly two decades."

SM: "Did the doctor sue? I would have."

DB: "I honestly do not know. But, I'll bet the ACLU heard about it."

SM: "Okay, let's get back to that profile."

CHAPTER FOURTEEN -
THE PROFILE AND THE LAW

DB: "Dr. Dailey told the Task Force the only way our system would pass legal muster was a multi-step procedure with the profile as the initial phase. Information gathered before passengers got to the boarding gate, at the time they got their tickets, and even before they boarded, had to be combined with modem technology to be what he described as a screening system that 'is both *maximally effective* and *minimally intrusive.*' In my first book, Dr. Dailey asserted that 'since the system used today is *minimally effective* but *maximally intrusive,* it is a farce because innocent nonthreatening airline passengers are subjected to long and unnecessary personal searches.'"

SM: "You tested his profile, I assume, because it was just a theory."

DB: "That theory, as you term it, gained the approval of the American Civil Liberties Union because the profile did not involve 'racial screening.' In addition, a New York Federal Court judge ruled that Dr. Dailey's profile did not violate the Fourth Amendment to the Constitution."

SM: "Isn't that the one dealing with search and seizure? Explain that court ruling."

DB: "Actually, there are two key court decisions. The one you are referring to was the case of *United States of America v. Frank Lorenzi Lopez.* Lopez and a companion, Gonzales, were about to board a Pan

American Airways flight out of JFK International Airport headed for Puerto Rico on November 14, 1970 when a gate agent determined the two men fit enough of Dr. Dailey's profile to be detained. Also, the two men set off the magnetometer. They then refused to produce valid identification. Following our tested procedure, the men were ordered back through the detector. Again, they set if off. Lopez and his friend were taken to a private area where they were 'patted down.' Although no weapons were found, a plastic envelope under Lopez's clothing turned out to be heroin."

SM: "What set off the detector?"

DB: "Lopez's friend had a small bag, which apparently contained some metal. But, there was nothing suspicious in it."

SM: "So, what was there in this court case that resulted in such an important ruling?"

DB: "Of all the ironies, the Pan Am service manager on his own issued a memorandum four months earlier to what he called 'updating' Dr. Dailey's list of characteristics. However, in doing so, the manager eliminated one of the fundamental characteristics of potential hijackers that Dr. Dailey had described privately to the judge, and added one that introduced what the record stated was 'an ethnic element ... raising serious equal protection problems. That added element called for individual judgment.' As a result, the judge ruled that the seized heroin could not be considered evidence."

SM: "Are you telling me the ruling turned on a technicality?"

DB: " Yes, but - and that is a big but - the judge ruled that the effect of the changes 'was to destroy the essential neutrality and objectivity of the approved profile.' In other words, the judge validated Dr. Dailey's profile as long as there were no changes to it. Also, the judge explained that Dr. Dailey's profile 'can be a valuable and effective method of protecting millions of air travelers from the threat of violence and sudden death in the air.'"

SM: "That's quite a decision."

DB: "Ironically, Pan Am had the right idea in applying Dr. Dailey's profile as Step One. The airline just messed with a procedure that, to repeat myself, we tested at various airports."

SM: "You said there were two key cases. What was the other one?"

DB: "I found the courthouse library a fountain of information, as the saying goes, and the librarians were wonderful helpers once I announced I was not an attorney. That is how I discovered the case of *Terry v.* Ohio. According to court documents, on October 31, 1963, Cleveland detective Martin McFadden claimed he saw two men presumably 'casing' a store. He approached the two men, told them he was a police officer, and asked their names. One was John W. Terry, and the other Richard Milton. When they seemed nervous, McFadden searched them for weapons, which they both had. He arrested them for carrying concealed weapons, and they later were sentenced to three years in prison. Terry appealed his conviction, arguing through his attorney that his arrest violated the Fourth Amendment to the Constitution regarding search and seizure. The appeal went to the U.S. Supreme Court, which ruled that the officer was within his rights because he had 'reasonable suspicion that the person stopped is committing a crime, or is about to.' To me, the vital words in that decision are 'reasonable suspicion.' Remember that the *Lopez* decision turned on a technicality - that the gate agent had changed a vital element in Dr. Dailey's profile. This overrode the proper 'reasonable suspicion' exercised by the gate personnel. Had the profile not been significantly changed, the verdict would have been very different. In my book, I cited the 1973 Federal American Law Review noting, 'Had the decision to stop and frisk (Lopez and Gonzalez) been made solely on the basis of activating the magnetometer, the court might have reached a different result.' In kind of a reverse finding, the judge on the one hand agreed that the *Terry* decision was properly applied, but without proper 'reasonable suspicion' either by Dr. Dailey's proper profile or the metal detector, he had no choice but to agree that any evidence found on the defendants had to be suppressed. And, once that evidence could not be used, Lopez won his appeal."

SM: "There must be other cases dealing with the Fourth Amendment and passenger search."

DB: "Lots. In *Chandler v. Miller,* the case revolved around a Georgia law requiring candidates for state office to pass a drug test.

Miller refused to take one, claiming it was in essence a search without suspicion. The U.S. Supreme Court agreed with his appeal."

SM: "Well, if suspicion has to be the first element for a constitutional search, how does that relate to airline passenger screening?"

DB: "Excellent question. I wondered about that myself. I felt that ordering every airline passenger to be searched only on the basis of setting off the magnetometer was improper. That goes back to Dr. Dailey's profile. We felt that if a passenger fit at least half a dozen elements of the profile, that was basis for suspicion. In fact, we referred to them as 'suspects.' Only then did we feel the authorities could go to the next steps of the total security system. And, when we discovered that no more than 2 percent of Eastern passengers tested, we concluded the proper search procedure would not impede the prompt boarding of the other 98 percent. The Final Report noted that Pan American World Airways, Trans World Airlines, and Continental Airlines later began to use the screening system. 'Of the first 226,000 passengers screened by those three airlines, some 1,268 selectees were identified for *further checking*. This is something more than one-half of 1 percent. Of those, only 638 failed the magnetometer test and required interviews. Thus, only 28/100th of 1 percent of total passengers screened required an interview following profile and magnetometer application. Of those interviewed, over half were able to provide a satisfactory explanation for high magnetometer readings. The balance, 304, submitted to search voluntarily. Of the 638 interviewed, 24 were denied boarding - and most were placed under arrest for offenses relating to narcotics or concealed weapons violations.'"

SM: "That's pretty convincing statistical evidence."

DB: "By the same token, Dr. Dailey and I feel that the number of suspected Mideast terrorists could be only a fraction of 1 percent of the total flying public, and thus easier to set them aside for further search and interrogation. Little did I realize, until I did further research, that President Bush has the authority to get around that 'suspicion' requirement because of the conflicts in the Middle East."

SM: "Did you get legal support, like from the Department of Justice?"

DB: "As the Final Report noted, in March 1969, the Department notified the FAA that our proposed screening procedure, with the profile as Step One, 'appeared reasonable and would be full endorsed by its Criminal Division.' Not only that, but the Division as well as the U.S. Marshals Service, which comes under the Department, pledged full cooperation in providing liaison and assistance."

SM: "What about the FBI?"

DB: "We tried to get the FBI to take part in the screening and searching of passengers, but it refused. Instead, U.S. marshals readily accepted that role."

SM: "Were there other legal aspects bearing on search?"

DB: "In November 2001, the Senate Republican Policy Committee issued a lengthy press release aimed at the American Civil Liberties Union. It stated that in the Spring of 1973, the ACLU 'adopted an official policy that opposed the present and previous systems of airport searches because they violate the requirements of the Fourth Amendment.' As stated before, the ACLU approved Dr. Dailey's profile, but apparently it did not like the current search procedure. The release cited the ACLU as opposing 'the current practice of searching the persons and belongings of all individuals' as inconsistent with the Fourth Amendment.' Notice the emphasis on all. We got approved because we opposed searching everyone."

CHAPTER FIFTEEN -
THE PROFILE AND FLEXIBILITY

SM: "So, if I understand you, the profile is what should provide the suspicion, not the magnetometer?"

DB: "In the interest of focusing on the most likely 'suspects,' absolutely yes.

SM: "And, if the most likely 'suspects' as you put it now are Mideast terrorists, that is why you and Dr. Dailey advocate changing the profile to meet the times?"

DB: " Absolutely! But, it has to be done using common sense. The Council on Foreign Relations published a paper posing this question: 'Do suicide terrorists fit a common profile?'"

SM: "What was the answer?"

DB: "The analogy of the Japanese kamikaze attacks during World War II is one answer. While our country had not experienced suicide terrorism on our soil as it pertains to aircraft hijacking prior to 9/11, certainly such terrorism in the Mideast should have alerted the U.S. to the possibility of such events happening to us. After all, terrorists bombed the World Trade Center in the early 1990's. That is why I said that disbanding the Task Force destroyed the historical connection between our work during 1969-70 and events three decades later."

SM: "So, you felt the new Office should have just continued on with what you began."

DB: "Since I was not part of that Office, I cannot say for sure. However, from what I understand, what eventually became the Office of Civil Aviation Security essentially was a 'cop shop.' Where the Task Force operated pretty much on its own, the new Office probably was a typical bureaucratic creation. The FAA has the reputation for being very passive until being pushed to do something. The attitude seems to be not to rock the boat, and do just enough to get a decent annual performance rating for shuffling paperwork. Eventually, it folded into the newly created Transportation Security Administration, part of the Department of Homeland Security."

SM: "By 1978, it must have seen your Final Report with its predictions."

DB: "You would think so. When I was researching my first book, I called that Office to ask that question. One person told me, 'Yeah, I've read it.' When I asked, 'Why didn't you dust it off when the World Trade Center was bombed in the early 1990's?' his reply was, 'Not my responsibility.' I will guarantee you that had our group been kept together, we would have been reviewing it constantly, especially those predictions. We were very proactive."

SM: "That sounds self-serving."

DB: "Of course I am biased. Dr. Dailey and I are angry that the FAA just sat there virtually doing nothing when the agency had in its hands a Manual of our work with those predictions. By destroying our link the past, the 'cop shop' would not know how flexible we were. For example, by going to those nine airports we discovered a variety of airport gates and a variety of types of passengers. Dr. Dailey always said his profile had to be adjusted from time to time. That is flexibility. I rest my case on that subject."

SM: "The 'cop shop' or whatever you call it must be doing something right."

DB: "Yes, of course. The screening per se is something right. However, no one has remembered that our approach not only was to spot 'suspects' but equally as important to facilitate boarding of 'innocent' passengers. Dr. Dailey and I have tried to contact almost all levels of government to help out on that. But, to no avail. That is why I am doing these books, in the hope that it is not too late to get proper passenger screening back to where it is efficient. Allow me to create a scenario that relates to what we have been saying."

SM: "I'm listening."

CHAPTER SIXTEEN -
THE GOOD, THE BAD, AND THE UGLY

DB: "The line of passengers waiting at the security station at Dulles International Airport was backed up. Screeners were focused on a white-haired woman in her 80's who slowly passed through the metal detector. The alarm went off, and she was told to go back through. She slowly returned to the front of the device and went through once more. The device sounded again."

"'Oh, dear,' she said to a screener. 'What did I do?'

"'Ma'am,' the screener said, 'go over that search area. A female officer will take you behind a curtain, where you should begin to ... ah ... disrobe.'

"The woman seemed confused. 'Why do I have to do that?' she asked, continuing to stand in front of the detector so no one else could get through.

"'Ma'am, you're holding up the line. Officer, please escort this woman so we can get the line moving.'

"A very overweight male officer took her elbow and directed to a small area to what looked like a curtained voting booth. A female office soon appeared and said, 'Please go inside and take off your outer clothing and shoes. I'll be back in a minute.' The now frightened woman did as she was told. A moment later, the female officer stepped inside the booth with her electronic wand, a hand-held version of the large metal detector. She ran the wand up and down the woman's body when it suddenly began to beep shrilly. 'Whatcha got there, honey?' the officer asked. 'Oh, dear,' she replied, 'that must be my pacemaker. I do have a note from my doctor in my purse.' The officer ignored the response and finally finished the scan, including the shoes. 'Okay, you can get dressed now and go on through,' she explained.

"The woman's 90-year-old husband, who had been right behind her in line, was having his own troubles. He too set off the alarm. The same burly officer led him to another search area, where he would be put through the same procedure his wife had experienced. The hefty officer's wand screeched almost immediately. 'Oh, my,' the man said, 'I have a hip replacement. I have a note from my doctor. . .' The officer was not interested and ran the wand along the man's shoes. Again it screeched. 'What's in your shoes, old man?' the officer asked. 'Oh, that's my lift. I was born with one foot shorter than the other, and my doctor told me to have a steel piece put into the heel to even me out. But, that threw 'my hip out of joint, so that's why...'

"The officer walked away and called to his supervisor, who also did a scan with the same results. The two officers whispered to one another until the supervisor said, 'Sir, let's see some photo ID.' The man fumbled through his pants that lay crumpled on the floor and finally found his card from the senior citizens development where he and his wife lived. The supervisor looked at it closely, then at the man, then at the ID, then at the man. Finally, he called over to the shift captain. After yet another whispered conference, the captain said, 'Sorry to inconvenience you, sir, but you know that ever since that shoe bomber incident, we can't be too careful. You're free to go and join your wife.'

"As he dressed, the man did not have any idea who or what a shoe bomber was. Rejoining his wife, who was now trembling, they slowly walked down the concourse to their departure gate."

SM: "You ought to be writing for television, or the movies."

DB: "Actually, part of that was based on a true incident a neighbor of ours encountered."

SM: "Any other incidents?"

DB: "Here is more of what New York Times columnist Joe Sharkey reported in his May 3, 2005 piece: At the Albuquerque, NM Airport, a passenger had her 6-month-old infant in her arms when she was stopped and told to remove her long-sleeve shirt, although she said others in line were not told to do so. She was taken aside. While she was subjected to a full body search, she said her infant also got a 'pat-down' as well. Then, there was the elderly woman at the Springfield, MO Airport in a wheelchair who was told to remove her shoes and 'every piece of outer wear, including her sweater.' Then, she was wheeled through the metal detector. Finally, one woman passenger refused to remove her shoes. She finally did after getting an additional inspection. Then, as she walked to her gate, she said she noticed a 'plainclothes guy doing his best imitation of a surfer, except for his military posture and the earpiece wire poking out from his ski cap.'"

SM: "Those might be exceptions to the rule."

DB: "I am not sure anyone tracks complaints because most people just want to get to their destinations and be done with it, so they assume there is some rationale behind such treatment."

CHAPTER SEVENTEEN - NO REPEAT OF 9/11

SM: "I understand you have made a number of observations about terrorism in general. I don't remember seeing or hearing you on any television talk shows. I can accept the fact that you have unique knowledge of airline passenger screening. But, aren't you going a bit far afield? For example, I understand that in a speech you gave on this subject, you said you doubted that there would be a repeat of 9/11."

DB: "That came in response to a question from someone in the audience. Truth be told, he was a skeptic about our program. In fact, he said he did not agree with one thing I said, and called me 'dangerous.' I said I felt strongly that Mideast terrorists would not try that method again. In a nutshell, there are many, many more what we used to call in the Army **targets of opportunity** on U.S. soil with a lot less risk than in trying again to hijack airplanes and divebomb them into buildings. We are such an open, and sometimes naive, society that we cannot hope to cover every possible target, the same way we cannot cover every one of the 30,000 daily flights in this country with armed sky marshals. Besides, those terrorists have a more immediate goal in Iraq and Afghanistan. And, as dysfunctional as our current system is, it still is a deterrent."

SM: "But, how do you account for the tragedies in London?"

DB: "If nothing else, that was in Europe where terrorists have the makings and the opportunities for suicide bombings. Also, London was totally unprepared for what happened. I am not saying that in a negative way. The point I am trying to make is that those terrorists, whether directly or indirectly connected with Al Qaeda, have a whole range of **targets of opportunity** with a risk of being caught less than trying to hijack an airplane."

SM: " Are you saying we are totally fair game?"

DB: "In a sense, yes. To my way of thinking, Mideast terrorists will keep doing their evil deeds until the risk factor is too great And, that goes for suicide bombings. But, I think we lose sight of the fact that such horrific events are as much propaganda for the dissident world as they are for us. One of my observations is that I feel Mideast terrorists are winning the psychological war. The very realization that they can strike anywhere in the world, even killing or maiming innocent adults and children, is chilling. Look at how many alerts have us near panic. So, what I am saying is that I feel those terrorists are looking at those other opportunities."

SM: "And, what are some of those so-called **targets of opportunity?**"

DB: "I think I would be guilty of disservice if I got specific. I can tell you this much. A number of people in the audiences where I have appeared have offered their own specifics. But, that begs another question. Can the U.S. exhibit the same resolve and resiliency the Londoners showed? Don't forget that London survived horrendous Nazi air strikes. We have not had to do that. Having said that, I like to quote President Franklin D. Roosevelt's famous words, 'The only thing we have to fear, is fear itself.' That is why I plead for sensible and effective antiterrorist programs that we can have confidence in."

SM: "In mid-2005, terrorists seemed to focus on bombing mass transit vehicles."

DB: "Not only that, but they kept up the pressure in Iraq and Afghanistan, and even turned to Egypt. From a tactical viewpoint, that points up the advantage those terrorists have over us. They know where to strike next, while we have to wait for the event to happen. They are not fighting fair. But, that is guerilla warfare, and as I said before, that is a type of warfare we are not used to fighting. I remember reading an article stating that the terrorists do not seem to have any problem in obtaining recruits, although there are reports that they have used coercion. That does not bother them. They will use any means to obtain their objective."

SM: "But, that's just your point of view."

DB: "The New York Times columnist Thomas Friedman also has the same point of view. In an April 13, 2005 piece, he noted: 'I've always believed that one of the most important reasons there has been no new terrorist attack in America has to do with the U.S. invasions of both Iraq and Afghanistan. To the extent that the (enemy) have a coordinated strategy (in those two countries), their first priority, I think, is to defeat American forces in the heart of their world. Because if they can defeat America in the heart of the Arab-Muslim world, it will have so much more resonance than setting off a car bomb in Las Vegas - especially now that 9/11 has set the terrorism bar so high in terms of effect.' He went on to say that if Iraq can form a freely elected government, 'that may signal the ... insurgency is being gradually defeated.... I fear that when and if the Jihadists conclude that they have been defeated in the heart of their world ... they may want to launch a spectacular, headline-grabbing act of terrorism in America that tries to mask, and compensate for, just how defeated they have become at home.'"

SM: "That's a pretty strong statement that seems to coincide with your views."

DB: "A friend of mine once said, 'If the Mideast terrorists want to make a statement, and they don't care about another 9/11, they might just try to attack a State Fair.'"

SM: "That's a scary speculation."

DB: "As I said, before they are too many easier targets of opportunity for Mideast terrorists if are as desperate as Friedman suggests. Should we stop the New Year's Eve celebration at Times Square? Should we stop the July 4th celebration on the national capital's Mall? Should we stop all athletic events? The list is endless. My answer is an emphatic NO! As Friedman ended his column, 'Let's stay extra vigilant at home.'"

CHAPTER EIGHTEEN - THE DOLLAR DRAIN

SM: "I understand another observation is that the conflicts in Iraq and Afghanistan are draining us financially."

DB: "More correctly, I said I feel Mideast terrorism has succeeded in diverting billions of U.S. dollars from our domestic needs. I am not an economist by any stretch of the imagination, but I understand the need to balance the books of our nation. Using money for the military is vital, but it must be used wisely. We cannot ignore major internal problems at the cost of funding a seemingly unending conflict. I am reminded of U.S. Senator J. William Fulbright of Arkansas. If my memory is correct, this brilliant man, who lent his name not only to highly sought academic scholarships but many political accomplishments, was defeated by then Arkansas Governor Dale Bumpers because he was accused of spending too much time away from his home state and from the people who elected him."

SM: "And, as I have asked before, your point is?"

DB: "The point is that we can be rich on the global front, but poor on the domestic front. Trying to balance the two is a monumental task. From what I read and hear, this teeter-totter cannot remain balanced forever. I think one way to help with the balance is to redirect our antiterrorism activities in a more productive way. Just throwing more and more money at homeland security is not the answer. As with a successful business, there has to be fiscal accountability in those efforts. Yes, I am talking dollars and sense ... s-e-n-s-e, not c-e-n-t-s

... if you forgive the pun. I admit I am not a historian, but I will bet there are plenty of examples where so much money went for foreign warfare at the expense of needs of the folks back home that people rebelled. I am not implying anyone will rebel, because that would denigrate the loss of military lives."

CHAPTER NINETEEN -
AIRBORNE DISTRACTIONS

SM: "Let's get back once more to the profile, because another question just popped into my head about armed sky marshals versus an armed cockpit crew."

DB: "More are those who have argued that either arm one or the other, but not both. Besides, gunplay at 35,000 should be avoided unless the circumstances do not leave any alternative."

SM: "You said armed sky marshals could not be on every flight. Were there any on the 9/11 flights?"

DB: "No. Boston, where two of the flights left from, had not had hijackings for many, many years. Personally, I am very opposed to the theory that having such personnel on certain flights, but not others, is a viable deterrent. Anyone could easily figure out the chances of catching a Mideast terrorist this way presents worse odds than trying to win the Lottery. My first book cited the FAA's own Bureau of Transportation Statistics concluding that there are 677,000 to 878,00 what are called 'revenue departures' a month. That does not take into consideration small private planes or even cargo planes. The numbers just are not there."

SM: "Are you saying armed sky marshals are not worth it?"

DB: "What I am saying is that I do not think that is a realistic alternative. If Mideast terrorists were able to board a plane, I submit that an armed sky marshal would not deter them. Let me give you this scenario. Let's take one of those 9/11 flights with five Mideast terrorist hijackers on board. One of those terrorists would make a commotion, enough to alert an armed sky marshal if one were aboard. Now, the terrorists knew they were home free."

SM: "Oh, come on. Where did you make that up from?"

DB: "When my wife and I were in Nice, France years ago, an elderly small woman with a baby in her arms came up to us begging for some money. While I was trying to shoo the woman away, I suddenly turned around to find a young boy standing next to me with his hand in my pocket. In another second or two, he would have had my passport. Or, if you prefer, such diversions are the stock and trade for magicians."

SM: "This all sounds as if we don't have a chance at dealing with terrorist hijackers once the plane is in flight."

DB: "I think that is an oversimplification. But, I repeat myself when I say the odds of dealing with such people shift from being in our favor on the ground to being in their favor once the plane is in the air. And, the latter becomes worse if you have suicide terrorists, who will give up their own lives, and take the lives of others, to accomplish their mission."

SM: "You've made your point."

DB: "One last item. The situation in the air gets worse on behemoth aircraft like a B-747 which has double decks. The terrorists could create a diversion on the upper deck, and drawing armed guards away from the main cabin. And, today, even larger aircraft are coming into service."

SM: "Well, if you don't have enough sky marshals to go around, what's wrong with telling the public they could be on certain flights?"

CHAPTER TWENTY - RANDOM IS AS RANDOM DOES

DB: "I certainly am not a psychologist, but it seems to me if you go that certain flights route, you are raising false hope. And, let's say, a plane is hijacked and passengers and crew are killed, but the flight did not have a sky marshal aboard. I am not sure I would trust that airline again. What could a sky marshal, or even two, have done on those 9/11 flights? As I said, if I were one of the terrorists, I would have made sure we identified that armed officer. But, let's go a step further and talk about pre-boarding random searches."

SM: "Please do."

DB: "After that Philadelphia incident, I wrote a letter to the Transportation Security Administration complaining about my random search. Here is part of that response: 'This random element prevents potential terrorists from beating the system by learning how it operates. Leaving out anyone group, such as senior citizens or the clergy, would remove the random element from the system and undermine security. We simply cannot assume that all future terrorists will fit any particular profile.'"

SM: "That sounds as if the TSA does not think much of your profile."

DB: "You got that right. By the same token, I would like to ask the TSA just how many terrorists has that agency caught under its random search procedure. I also would like to know just how the security people decide just who is subject to that random search. It is ludicrous to believe any of the 9/11 terrorists could have been deterred by the prospect of being picked at random to be searched. Do the Iraqi terrorists stop bombing vehicles because they are in an armed convoy?"

SM: "Obviously you do not think much of random searching."

DB: "Not at the cost of humiliating passengers for no good reason. Don't just take my word for it. In my book, I cited a comment by noted columnist and television talk show panelist Charles Krauthammer: 'Random searches are a ridiculous charade ... that not only gives a false sense of security, but, in fact, diminishes security because it wastes so much time and effort on people who are obviously no threat. Random searches are being done purely to defend against the charge of racial profiling.' Dr. Dailey responded to Krauthammer in a letter to the editor this way: 'Racial and ethnic screening can only produce illegal search.' There even are those who argue that random searches violate the Fourth Amendment to the Constitution. Remember, the Federal Court judge upheld Dr. Dailey's profile because it did not involve racial screening."

SM: "Surely there is some good to random searching, or the TSA would have abandoned it."

DB: "I think here is where you have to understand the bureaucracy. Once a program is put in motion, you would have to move heaven on earth to stop it. It is like a freight train that suddenly has gone out of control, and no one knows how to stop it. The Council on Younger Lawyers of the Federal Bar Association noted in its 1968 handbook on the Bill of Rights that personal search is allowed 'so long as it was reasonable.' I would like to hear how the TSA defines 'reasonable.' What was 'reasonable' about me to require the only search on a flight? I did not have any dangerous weapon on me or in my carry-on. Anything else about me would fall into the racial or ethnic categories. Let me cite another source that I used in my other book. W.R. LaFave is a widely known and respect writer on legal matters. He cited a slew of cases in his 3rd edition of *Search and Seizure*. He supported use of the profile as Step One. But, he went even further: 'The anti-hijacking system (of ours) is unusual in that it provides statistics showing the precise probabilities involved.' Also, LaFave pointed out that most passengers do not know that they can refuse to be searched, but will be denied boarding. However, that certainly raises suspicion."

SM: "So, you absolutely insist on the profile being Step One."

DB: "If you rely primarily on the metal detector, I submit the device only is as effective as the person operating it. There have been many stories about how easily scanners get bored. Much effort has been put into replacing the magnetometer with more sophisticated electronics. In a March 11, 2003 editorial, however, The New York Times stated that 'the creating of a highly intrusive federal surveillance program raises serious privacy and due process concerns.' LaFave cited the case of *United States v. Albarado* in which the ruling stated that use of the magnetometer alone 'would not serve any valid purpose as a high percentage of passengers activate the device even if carrying innocuous items.' La Fave went on to say: 'It by no means follows, however, that the screening authorities should immediately proceed to frisk a person who has activated the magnetometer. Such a procedure would deprive the hijacker detection system of a characteristic which is essential to it being deemed a reasonable administrative search, namely, that the intrusions are no more severe than is necessary to produce acceptable results.' Now, that opens another can of legal worms because of the many ways the term 'acceptable results' can be defined. All in all, there are as many court cases on one side of the issue as there are on the other."

SM: "Do I infer from what you just said the justification for a personal search can be based solely on setting off the magnetometer?"

DB: "Yes, but you have to remember that the President has the authority to approve such search under the 'war' powers Congress granted the President."

SM: "Are you implying the government is relying too much on electronics?"

DB: "The government keeps trying. The latest is called a 'puffer,' that allows screeners to find nonmetallic bombs without physically inspecting passengers."

SM: "What have you got against such devices?"

DB: "I'm not against devices. I'm against using them as Step One to screen every single passenger. In the American Psychologist magazine of February 1975, Dr. Dailey and his colleague, Dr. Evan W. Pickrel, discussed the psychological contributions to defenses against hijacking. They asserted that of the 30 hijackings between January 1970 and February 1971, '87 percent would have been stopped at the boarding gate if the (Task Force) screening procedures had been used, but (they) were only voluntary at that time.' Think about that. The profile could have prevented almost 9 out of 10 hijackings. Yes, electronics is important, but only if they are used in conjunction with the profile."

SM: "I must admit that is impressive."

DB: "The article also noted that 'following World War Two, an airline in Alaska used to frisk passengers on some of its flights and take away all guns, knives, and alcoholic beverages. Many (of those) pilots carried guns as part of their regular flight equipment and (also) locked the cabin door. If passengers were heard to be fighting, the pilots sometimes donned oxygen masks and simply climbed to an altitude that put the passengers to sleep.'"

SM: "That is almost comical. But, I supposed, in Alaska anything can happen."

DB: "The Internet also provided me with another interesting comment A writer named Michael Hammerschlag wrote a piece titled 'Airline Security.' His observation was this: 'By definition, the chance that any single random security break is an actual terrorist is negligible, since terrorists are so infinitesimal a number.'"

SM: "The impression you champion is that privacy of the individual is more important than fighting potential terrorist hijacking."

CHAPTER TWENTY ONE -
PRIVACY VERSES SECURITY NEEDS

DB: "No, I am just trying to find a realistic balance between the two. Just to remind you, the American Civil Liberties Union approved of Dr. Dailey's approach because it did not involve an invasion of privacy. And, that was upheld in the New York Federal Court case. Then, there was a ruling on September 9, 2003 by U.S. District Court Judge Alvin Hellerstein in a suit filed by families of those killed or wounded in the World Trade Center suicide attacks. In upholding the families' right to sue not only the makers of the crashed aircrafts but also owners of the twin towers, Judge Hellerstein ruled that 'negligent security screening might have contributed to the deaths of 3,000 people.'"

SM: "Sounds to me like which came first, the chicken or the egg situation."

DB: "It is, but that is why we went out of our way to create a procedure that would meet security requirements, yet would necessarily abuse the right to privacy, the right to oppose improper searches. Frankly, I think current procedures have fallen into the trap of putting security ahead of privacy when there really has been a viable alternative for more than three decades."

SM: "What do the courts have to say about this Catch 22 dilemma?"

DB: "I did a lot of research on that and found that courts have not been in agreement with one another. The right to search was upheld in the famous *Terry v. Ohio* case where the Supreme Court ruled that a policeman could frisk a person if he were convinced it was needed to 'protect himself and others from possible danger.' My nonlegal focus is on the words 'if he were convinced.' In my frisk at Philadelphia that I described earlier, no 'convincing' was involved; I was merely picked out because, as the security officer admitted, 'we have to search at least one person on each flight.' Was my privacy improperly invaded? You betcha."

SM: "But, you are not a lawyer."

DB: "As the old joke goes, 'no, I'm not, but I have other good habits.' Let me cite you another court ruling I used in my previous book. In *United States v. Scott*, the Supreme Court ruled that 'searches are to be judged by a standard of objective reasonableness.' Here we go on a legal technicality. Because of 9/11, our country went to war with Mideast terrorists. As such, it tacitly ordered everyone to be searched as a defense against further such acts. The argument is whether that meant the Fourth Amendment to the Constitution only covered 'peaceful' times when the right to privacy and protection against improper searches and seizures could take place. I certainly am not a qualified legal person, but I submit a tried and true search system could prevent such dilemmas. However, let me play devil's advocate. In my book, I cited another case, *United States v. Skipworth*, which concluded that 'reasonableness does not require that officers search only those who meet (the) FAA personality profile or who manifest signs of nervousness or who otherwise appear suspicious.' Just to flip the legal coin back again, I cited the case of *United States v. Cyzewski* that ruled that 'airport searches are reasonable insofar as they permit government agents to determine whether (a) suspect presents (an) immediate danger to air commerce.'"

SM: "So, who's right and who's wrong?"

DB: "That is not for me to say. Again, what I do say is to the point of boring repetition is that Dr. Dailey's profile, and the system's step-by-step procedure, avoids this dilemma because suspicion is raised through at least half a dozen behavioral characteristics. Did

I exhibit at least half a dozen of those characteristics? No, yet I was singled out for search. Did that 80-year-old woman exhibit at least half a dozen of those characteristics? No, yet she was singled out for search only because her pacemaker set off the magnetometer. Did her 90-year-old husband . . ."

SM: "Okay, okay. In all honesty, we are aware of some, shall we say, inappropriate procedures used by security personnel."

DB: "Some of those problems are due to the personnel themselves. Some are due to the equipment. A July 9, 1985 story in The New York Times quoted a security expert Robert W. Deichert as saying, 'The equipment and procedures are available to stop hijackings and terrorism, but they are not applied adequately, nor is common sense.' Another security expert, Henry P. Reis-El Bara, said, 'The technology is there. The problem is that as in many other things, the security at airports is oriented more toward crisis management than long-term vigilance.' The article went on to assert that some security devices 'are too often poorly operated or maintained, that security quality varies widely, that the weakest links in the system are personnel responsible for security, that new technology is delayed because of lack of funding, and that the risk of terrorism can never be eliminated.' Then, there is the observation in our Final Report on Page 6 'that human error or carelessness in use of deterrents might permit a hijacker to slip through the course of obstacles.'"

SM: "Don't I recall a General Accounting Office issuing a critical report on airport screening?"

DB: "I read that in The Washington Post. The September 2003 article stated that 'the federal government isn't testing the skills of airport security screens as thoroughly as it did before the Sept. 11, 2001 terrorist attacks and needs to develop a recurring training program. But, to be fair, there are times when security people do their job right.'"

SM: "What was that?"

DB: "A family had been vacationing in Orlando, Florida. With their luggage piled up waiting for transportation to the airport, a young girl walked up to them and said she had been given a stuffed teddy bear but that she could not keep it. She handed it to the family's child. The family, in a hurry, accepted it. At the airport, the child had to place the teddy bear on the conveyor belt. Suddenly, the alarm went off. One of the officers looked in amazement at his screen where he could clearly see a .22-caliber gun sewn inside the bear. On being questioned, the parents relayed the story of the 'gift.' They were cleared. While finding a weapon is not unusual, this was considered out of the ordinary. And, this happened despite constant warnings from security personnel that passengers never should accept anything from a stranger."

SM: "I apologize, but again, I have other commitments. However, I want to continue our interview, extended as it has become. Next time, I would like to talk about why hijackers hijack."

DB: "I want to be as helpful as I can, regardless of the time involved."

CHAPTER TWENTY TWO - MIDEAST TERRORIST MOTIVATION

SM: "I did not realize there were so many sides to this hijacking and terrorism issue. I did get a chance to read your book, and I am intrigued about the chapter on hijacker motivations."

DB: " I wish Dr. Dailey were here to talk about that aspect. But, he has sent me a lot of material, and we have talked at length when I visited him down in Culpeper, Virginia."

SM: "Give it a try, anyhow. I sense this could be an important key."

DB: "We have to separate motivations of past hijackings headed mostly to Cuba from the one horrific devastation of 9/11. That is why Dr. Dailey insisted that his profile, and even the magnetometer, needed to be flexible enough to adjust to the times."

SM: "Let's use that as a starting point."

DB: "As Dr. Dailey noted in the previous book, the first officially reported aircraft hijacking attempt took place on February 21, 1930 in Peru. The first U.S. aircraft hijacking took place on May 1, 1961 aboard a flight from Miami to Key West, Florida. In between those incidents, and then later up until the Task Force came into being, the majority of the hijackings were politically motivated. A few others were for criminal reasons, especially the one involving the infamous Dan (alias D.B.) Cooper. On Thanksgiving eve of 1971 - remember that was more than a year after the Task Force had been disbanded

- a passenger by that name boarded a Northwest Orient B-727 in Portland, Oregon. The plane had hardly gained altitude when he sent a note to the captain that he had a bomb and threatened to blow up the aircraft unless he was given $200,000 and four parachutes. The plane was diverted to the Seattle-Tacoma Airport. His demands were met, and the plane took off for what he said was his destination - Mexico."

SM: "Now I remember the case. Didn't he parachute out of the plane and never was found?"

DB: "Correct. He bailed out somewhere over the state of Washington. His body never was located, and stories abounded. Some say he died; some say he disappeared into the wilderness. There even was a movie made of the incident."

SM: "Well, at least he was not headed to Cuba."

DB: "Who knows what was on his mind? But, the important point is this. Even if the Portland Airport had a security system, my guess is that Cooper would not have been stopped. Although we went to nine airports during our testing phase, Portland was not one of them. Who in the world ever would think a hijacker would do his deed in the northwest United States? An airport in that part of the country, or even in a small town anywhere, would not have the security diligence as, say, La Guardia, or Miami, or even Boston."

SM: " Are you saying trying to cover every airport in the U.S. is hopeless?"

DB: "What I am saying is that some airports are more lax than others. Besides, if all Cooper had was nerve, but not a bomb, he would have passed through easily. Many police departments are not willing to have victims give in to extortion, which is what this was. But, someone made the decision not to take a chance, and paid his demand."

SM: "Maybe he was not even questioned because that new Office at the FAA was not up and running yet to alert all airports."

DB: "An excellent point, although a year and a half had passed between when that Office took over for us, and Cooper got away with his bluff."

SM: "Okay. Let's get back to general motivations."

DB: "In the previous book, Dr. Dailey analyzed earlier worldwide hijackings and concluded that hijackers were a combination of what he called 'homesick Cubans, mentally ill, political terrorists, and even felons.' In his own book, *The Pioneer Heritage,* Dr. Dailey stated that hijackers want attention. 'The gratification apparently comes from an act of high drama representing one brief moment of power and glory in a lifetime of failure,' he wrote. That was a psychological analysis."

SM: "Could there also have been a psychiatric analysis also?"

DB: "You must have read a book titled *The Skyjacker* by Dallas psychiatrist David G. Hubbard published in 1971. I want to discuss him later. After interviewing 20 hijackers, Dr. Hubbard concluded they were 'effeminate, sexually inadequate, ineffectual, generally apolitical individuals who have skyjacked in situations of total personal failure.' He also interjected the possibility that hijackers were subjected to unusual gravity forces. His final conclusions were that hijackings could be controlled by an 'agreement for automatic repatriation,' by his medical research dealing with 'sexual inadequacy' of the hijacker, by adding women to the space program to diminish the notion that flight is 'a male prerogative,' elimination of the death penalty or long prison terms for captured hijackers, and conducting further research."

SM: "Sounds sort of like pie in the sky, if you forgive my own pun."

DB: "That's a good one. But, keep in mind that not one of his conclusions could be adapted to the same kind of airline passenger screening procedure as we produced. This was the same man who wanted Task Force members incarcerated at a mental institution because, as I recall, he felt we were 'nuts' trying to create a psychological profile."

SM: "Well, it's obvious what the motivations of the 9/11 terrorists were."

DB: "I only can give you my views. I am not a psychiatrist, nor a psychologist"

SM: "I'll accept that caveat.

DB: "Terrorism is nothing new. History is replete with various forms of terrorism, sometimes called barbarism. I looked up the definition of terror in the dictionary, and it was enlightening. For example, terror is defined as 'a state of intense fear; a frightening aspect; a cause of anxiety; an appalling thing.' But, the next definition is interesting: 'violent or destructive acts (as bombing) committed by groups in order to intimidate population or government into granting their demands.'"

SM: "Why did you find those last words interesting, as you put it?"

DB: "I think we all may have forgotten that the terrorists did have demands. They wanted the U.S. out of the Middle East, if nothing else. That gets back to my point about understanding the terrorist mind set. We tend to deal with other people around the world as if they were just like us. Terrorists are not like us by any stretch of the imagination. When Dr. Dailey created his profile, he did not presuppose the behavior of hijackers. But, once he did his research, then he had a behavior pattern. By the way, too many people interpret behavior as how people look and talk. That is so misguided. Behavior is a very complicated science, from what I have read. So, developing a behavior pattern only is as realistic as its testing. And, that is the basic fault Dr. Dailey and I find in current procedures."

SM: "Spell that out, please."

DB: "Since 9/11, decision makers have sped headlong into procedures without having done any research. The simplistic 'solution' to protecting us from another 9/11 was to search every passenger. Probably the most important conclusion our testing reached was that you can focus the major part of your anti-hijacking efforts on a manageable number of 'suspects.'"

SM: "Are you implying that since 9/11 the government should have focused on only 2 percent of the flying public?"

DB: "Mideast terrorists are not different from terrorists anywhere in the world. They have total disregard for their lives. They are tenacious in accomplishing their goals. A USA Today article in August 2003 contained two sentences that bear this out: 'Unlike many criminal networks, al-Qaeda seems to learn from its mistakes.

Some FBI officials believe the group identified flaws in the 1993 Trade Center garage bombing that killed six people, and then developed a more effective attack. What did they need? The ability to fly? They got that in flight training here. Money? They got that coming in from overseas. They spoke enough English to be able to rent cars and apartments. And they had the discipline to stay out of trouble. Investigators say they have no evidence the hijackers told anyone about their plot.'"

SM: "I know you have protected yourself by saying you are not expert in motivation. But; what is your take on all of this?"

DB: "Willingness of an enemy to die is not new. The Japanese for a long time during World War II would rather die than be captured. The Chinese in the Korean conflict were not afraid to conduct virtual suicide attacks on our troops. And, Vietnam was replete with stories of similar attacks. Then, we come to Iraq, and suddenly we seem to be surprised that an enemy is willing to die if he/she can take victims, whether military or civilian. I put that in the class of underestimating the enemy. The French certainly underestimated the Vietnamese rebels until they suffered a disaster at Dien Bien Phu that forced them to pull out. The Russians underestimated the Afghan rebels until they were forced to pull out. My point is that if you underestimate the enemy, you don't know how to deal with the enemy. I believe we underestimated, or even misunderstood, Mideast terrorism, or believed it would not spread here."

CHAPTER TWENTY THREE - WARNING FLAGS WERE IGNORED

SM: "How could we have known it would spread here and create 9/11?"

DB: "There actually were so many clues over the years that it staggers the mind. Let me start with an op ed piece in the March 27, 2004 issue of The New York Times by Peter R. Neumann. He is identified as a research fellow in international terrorism at the Department of War Studies, King's College, London. The last paragraph really sets the stage for my views: 'In the end, the 9/11 hearings are likely to find that intelligence failure that led to the horrific attacks stemmed from the longstanding problems of wrongly placed agents, failed communications between government departments and lack of resources. But it was also a failure of vision - one for which the current administration must take responsibility.'"

SM: "What's wrong with that conclusion? Sounds pretty lucid to me."

DB: "What's wrong are wrong conclusions. The blame placed on the current administration is wrong. At the risk of sounding like a parrot, the blame goes all the way back to August 1970 when the FAA disbanded the Task Force. You don't have to only blame intelligence and communication dysfunctions, although there were many. Lack of resources? We had the right resource from the get-go - Dr. Dailey's tested and verified profile. All else should have stemmed from that.

But, what happened instead? The Nixon administration panicked and ordered all airline passengers to be searched. In hindsight, this eventually played right into the hands of the current terrorists, because for the next three decades efforts to curtail hijackings were not focused on terrorism-related events. Screening yoyoed. There was no continuity because, as I said before, the link was broken because our warnings were ignored."

SM: "I assume you are referring to what was in the Task Force Final Report."

DB: "Exactly! What could be more clear than our use of the term **terrorists** way back in 1978? That is the real shame of 9/11 - totally ignoring what the Task Force concluded *could happen! Had that not been ignored, all the warning signs during the next more than two decades* **would** *have certainly alerted our decision makers!* If nothing else, and I repeat, if nothing else, the February 26, 1993 bombing of the World Trade Center should have set off every security seismograph in this country! I guess it was not important that only six people were killed, and more than 1,000 wounded. Perhaps this was because the bombing happened on the ground. You wouldn't have had to be a terrorism expert to connect the 1978 warnings with the 1993 incident."

SM: "Let me cut right to the chase. So, whom do you blame?"

DB: "I place the crucial blame on the FAA, but collateral blame on each administration from President Nixon through Presidents Ford, Carter, Reagan, the elder Bush, and Clinton, right up to the current Bush. Had the FAA alerted each administration, I feel history would have been very different today. To remind you, I said there were two vital mistakes - the first one that disbanded the Task Force and did not take advantage of its work, and 'Black September' which took away the focus on Dr. Dailey's profile as Step One of a viable screening procedure. And, I do not need to go into the tepid approach the FAA took to plenty of warning signs. When the FAA issued three information circulars to airports in 1998 of a possible terrorist hijacking along the East Coast, I cannot find any evidence that the agency brought back a modified profile as Step One. According to a Boston Globe story of May 26, 2002, 'Bush administration and

FAA officials have characterized the pre-September intelligence as too broad to defend against and said they lacked a credible hijacking threat.'"

SM: "Don't you think that under the circumstances the administration did all it could?"

DB: "No. To me, it was more of the same - keep on screening all passengers with primary reliance on the magnetometer, followed by making too many innocent people suspects. From all the information I have been able to glean, the profile could well have identified all 19 terrorists as 'suspects' because they fit enough of the profile to be detained. The fact that they somehow smuggled those box cutters on the flights is a secondary matter. What good would those weapons have been if those flights had taken off without the terrorists? The fact that some of the terrorists had faulty passports also is a secondary matter. I have to keep harping away at the assertion that 'suspects' had to raise more than just one warning flag."

SM: "Can you say that our administrations and the FAA were not aware of international incidents?"

DB: "I am sure they were. But, I must remind you that our Task Force had an excellent representative from the Office of International Aviation Affairs, Lee Jett. Dr. Reighard, our chairman, knew full well there had to be international implications. And, we did coordinate with the International Civil Aviation Organization (ICAO). If memory serves me correctly, we hoped that what we did would be a model for nations around the world. What good does it do for us to have security measures when foreign airports have different measures? We are getting into the field of geopolitics, and notice the Task Force did not have anyone representing that discipline. We wanted to stay outside of politics. Very few members of Congress really were interested in our work, or their staff members surely would have alerted those lawmakers about an impending crisis."

SM: "Let's bring the situation up to date. Won't you agree that a lot has been done to upgrade the screening process?"

CHAPTER TWENTY FOUR -
BUREAUCRACY BUMBLING

DB: "This really opens up a can of worms. At the outset, I will not deny my bias about this aspect."

SM: "Why do you take such a hard line?"

DB: "I must confess that Dr. Dailey and I virtually cried after 9/11 because we believed that had the work the Task Force did still been Step One, the catastrophe could have been prevented. But, we were trumped by bureaucracy. And, I believe I have covered that subject through your questions. And, look at the bureaucratic consequences of 9/11. We have a continuing military struggle in two Mideast countries. We have continuous rising numbers of casualties. We continue to pour billions of dollars into this effort. And, now we have yet another layer of bureaucracy - the Department of Homeland Security and all its subdivisions."

SM: "Let's pursue that aspect in more detail."

DB: "To do that, I want to cite an article in the March 11, 2003 issue of The New York Times, because it goes to the heart of this matter. Interestingly enough, this appeared in the business travel section."

SM: "Did you say business travel?"

DB: "Yes. I thought the columnist Joe Sharkey did a good job, but inadvertently identified the core of what is wrong. The column started off describing the first electronic background system called 'CAPPS

I.' That stood for 'Computer Assisted Passenger Prescreening System.' It was put into service in the later 1990's and adjusted after 9/11. In February 2003, the system was upgrade to 'CAPPS II.' As Sharkey explained it, the original system 'was designed to select passengers for extra security screening based on a number of undisclosed indicator criteria.' Sound familiar?"

SM: "I just know you're going to tell me that is Dr. Dailey's profile."

DB: "Sharkey then notes that 'CAPPS II has been partly designed to address the faults inherent in the original program, which has been at the heart of the much-discussed airport security hassle complaint that airlines blame for at least part of their drop in business travel revenue.' Sound familiar?"

SM: "Hmmm. Oh, yes. The Task Force made a point of developing a system that would not adversely affect airline revenue."

DB: "Good, so far. Sharkey goes on to describe a 'new computer-based system (that) will evaluate precise personal information about a passenger booking a ticket, and then assign that passenger one of three color-based security ratings.'"

SM: "Oh, yes - green for no problem, yellow for additional screening, and red for hold the phone you're in trouble."

DB: "It seems, according to the column, that privacy groups did not think much of 'CAPPS II.' And, they took it out on Delta Air Lines, which had volunteered to test the new program."

SM: "I'm with you so far, but I don't have a clue where you are going with this."

DB: "Both 'CAPPS' programs gathered information about Americans traveling on American planes, by and large."

SM: "So, what's wrong with that?"

DB: "But, *we are supposed to be looking for Mideast terrorists who might want to repeat 9/11. Instead, we are looking at innocent American travelers.*"

SM: "Maybe we were thinking those terrorists might have more of their kinds of people who are Americans."

DB: "If that were the case, then there should have been multiple 'CAPPS' systems - one to look for hardened Mideast terrorists, and another for Mideast terrorist 'moles.' Some of the original profile elements certainly can be included, others can be omitted, and new ones can be added."

SM: "Why haven't you and Dr. Dailey made your suggestions known to the right people?"

DB: "Lord knows, we have tried. We contacted the White House, Members of Congress, the Secretary of Homeland Security, the Administrator of the TSA, the Secretary of Transportation, the Administrator of the FAA, and members of both the electronic and print media. We have a perfect score - not one of those were interested. That is why this book is the last alternative."

SM: "Aren't you being provocative just to get attention?"

DB: "Whatever is provocative, to use your term, is based on fact, or personal observation based on my experience and background."

SM: "Aren't the 'CAPPS' systems a good way to spot potential Mideast terrorist hijackers?"

DB: "The Council on Foreign Relations issued a Q&A sheet on terrorism in 2003. One of the questions was, 'Do suicide terrorists fit a common profile?' The answer was: 'Experts used to think so, but after September 11, they are less sure. As Brian Jenkins of the RAND think tank has put it, typical Middle Eastern suicide bombers were usually thought to be poor, not very well educated, and possibly psychologically damaged young men in their early 20's. Experts used to argue that men who were older, better educated, and had more social status, would be less inclined to kill themselves. This would normally have been a good bet, but the September 11 attackers were older - particularly those who clearly knew it was to be a suicide mission. They had better educations and appear to have been far more sophisticated than their predecessors. The profile of suicide attackers now requires revision.'"

SM: "That is an interesting answer."

DB: "Here's another one. Question: 'Can suicide terrorism be prevented?' Answer: 'Experts say that if a competent terrorist organization can operate freely and keep its operations secret, stopping its suicide attacks may be extremely difficult.'"

SM: "It sounds more and more like we don't have a chance of preventing suicide attacks in this country."

DB: "As critical as I have sounded of the bureaucracy, I also am an optimist. If bureaucrats can be flexible, if they will reread our Final Report, and if they understand the approach we took with Dr. Dailey's profile, I firmly believe we can do the best we can. No, we cannot stop all attempts. We said that more than 30 years ago. But, at least we can do better. However, as I said before, suicide terrorism has to be dealt with at its origin, and that is beyond what we are talking about here. According to my military experience, and I am not a member of the Joints Chiefs of Staff by any means, you do not want to fight a war of attrition. That gives terrorists the advantage. They even can go underground for a while, and resurface when they feel the time is right. Fighting terrorism on rigid bureaucratic terms is a lesson in futility."

SM: "Let's continue to focus on the present with an eye toward the future."

CHAPTER TWENTY FIVE -
PRESENT TENSED-UP SITUATION

DB: "Remember that spate of airline cancellations in early 2004 because of terrorists scares? That is just what we wanted to avoid by having the upper hand in publicizing our efforts. And, that is why I claim one of the aims of terrorists is to hit us in the financial belly. Airlines depend a lot on business clients, and during early 2004 those clients decided not to fly as often."

SM: "But, hasn't that been turned around?"

DB: "Thank goodness, yes. Dysfunctional as screening is, it still presents an added obstacle to hijacking attempts. However, I have another view of this. I believe that Mideast terrorists now are concentrating on a guerilla war in Iraq and Afghanistan. That is using much of the terrorists' resources, not only in money but in lives. Besides, the 9/11 effort took a lot of time and planning."

SM: "I don't think I heard that take on terrorism before."

DB: "Again, I am not an expert in such matters, but I continue to look at things from what I think is the terrorist point of view. They have an agenda that can change with the wind. That is not to say we can afford to let our guard down. Quite the contrary. But, that begs the question of what is the most effective deterrent. I do not believe there is one particular deterrent. But, there is a lot that can be done. For example, sharing information seems all to simple an answer for what was a war of fiefdoms for many years regarding terrorism. At the risk of repeating myself, you have to understand the bureaucracy and its motto of protecting turf at all costs. Even within agencies you can find bureaucratic jealousies. When I worked at the Department of Justice, Attorney General Ramsey Clark was J. Edgar Hoover's boss. Maybe he was, on paper, but Hoover was his own boss of the FBI. I learned quickly that trying to get cooperation from the FBI was an exercise in patience."

SM: "I think we all know about Hoover and the FBI."

DB: "There continues to be controversy over how to react to tension. I saw on television that officials cannot figure out how to enforce the no-fly zone over the nation's capital. It seems there is not one central figure coordinating how to deal with private planes that enter that zone. It seems that at least on 350 occasions, military aircraft were 'scrambled' to escort those errant planes.

SM: "I guess we're entering the realm of sharing information."

DB: "That surely is a hot button topic. Zillions of words already have been spoken about the lack of same among intelligence gathering organizations. Currently, efforts have been centered around databases. The Terrorist Screening Center, run by the FBI, coordinates information throughout the government and even throughout industry. But, I have to keep repeating, that while such information about potential terrorism acts is useful, it translates into searching innocent Americans."

SM: "Are you implying this is useless?"

DB: "What I am implying is that such information would be useful if from it a credible screening system for *potential Mideast terrorists* can be developed. I know I am repeating myself, but there has to be two separate screening systems."

SM: "I seem to recall the Clinton administration allocated $300 million for counter-terror measures, better screening of airline passengers, more FBI agents to deal with airport security, and more bomb-sniffing animals."

DB: "That was the White House Commission on Aviation Safety and Security which Vice President Gore chaired. That group came into being following the July 1996 explosion of TWA Flight 800 over

Long Island Sound. President Clinton signed the allocation into law in October."

SM: "How can you not say that the government has been trying to do what it can to prevent a repeat of 9/11 ?"

DB: "That's a fair question. Government is doing a lot. But, Dr. Dailey and I maintain it is focused in the wrong direction. A story from WorldNetDaily in March 2002 asserted: 'A computerized system used by airlines to screen suspicious passengers failed to expose the 19 Arab hijackers on Sept. 11 because it omits key terrorist-profiling indicators such as national origin, a Federal Aviation Administration security official says. If airlines had profiled passengers based on human criteria, he says, the roughly 3,000 Americans who died that day might still be alive. If human-profiling was conduced on the terrorists who were made selectees that day, then maybe some or the entire plot could have been avoided.' The official was not named, only identified as working in the agency's Aviation Security Division. The system he referred to that CAPPS II. The official went on to say, 'CAPPS was developed because the airline industry didn't want to do human-profiling. Yet human-profiling is the single-biggest deterrent against terrorism in the aviation industry.' Pretty strong words, wouldn't you say?"

SM: "Can you assure me he is not one of your plants?"

DB: "In all honesty, I had never heard of the guy, and never knew his views until I got that story off the Internet"

SM: "Isn't there a concern over sharing information about passengers?"

DB: "The Washington Post in September 2003 reported the airline JetBlue admitting 'it violated its own privacy policy by supplying names, phone numbers and addresses of one million passengers to an Alabama company called Torch Concepts, which was working on an Army database to identify suspected terrorists. This has been a concern of civil libertarians for some time.'"

SM: "Don't I recall something about airlines being ordered to share such information?"

DB: "You're probably referring to another Post story three days later stating that TSA Administrator James A. Loy threatened 'to compel U.S. airlines to cooperate in handing over data about their passengers for a new government computer screening system, which has been widely criticized as violating privacy rights.' Loy was referring to CAPPS II. It never happened."

SM: "Then, there were those color codes."

DB: "Oh, yes. If you had a green card (a terrible pun), you aced the boarding process. If you got yellow, you got some extra interrogation. If you got red, you not only could not board the flight, but in all probability you had to face the law. Me, I'm red-green color blind. Seriously, this was just grasping at straws."

SM: "By the way, what did you think about that order that prevented you from going to the airplane restroom for 30 minutes after takeoff and 30 minutes prior to landing?"

DB: "Thank goodness that finally got rescinded. Forgive me, but that pissed me off. I had prostate cancer surgery some years ago, and that decreased the size of my bladder. I never know when I have to make a beeline for the john. And, I am sure there are others with worse problems than mine."

SM: "I think this is a good time for us to stop. I have some commitments for the next two days, so let's get together right after that"

DB: "See you then."

CHAPTER TWENTY SIX -
INTERNATIONAL IMPLICATIONS

SM: "There seems to be one area we barely touched on, and that is how other nations around the world deal with terrorism and hijackings."

DB: "I must confess all I know about this is what I read in the papers and hear and see on television. But, having been to Europe several times on vacation with my wife, I only can tell you about our experiences at various airports. I don't recall any of the major airports overseas requiring passengers to take off their shoes, or to have a lot of strip searches as we do here. That is not to say other nations do not take airport security seriously. On the contrary. We found that places like Heathrow in England and DeGaulle in France are thorough but fair in their security. Amsterdam was more relaxed, as was Helsinki, but still competent. Ironically, each airport has its own levels of what will set off the metal detectors."

SM: "I recall you had said that even in this country, each airline sets its own standards."

DB: " Yes. As I mentioned before, each country does the same. I ran across a December 2002 Internet story issued by BBC News that had some interesting comments. A top security consultant was quoted as saying 'it was essential that (armed) air marshals were backed up by improved security on the ground.'"

SM: "That sounds familiar."

DB: "The point is that virtually every country agrees with the Task Force's basic premise that the major focus of dealing with potential terrorist hijackers is to keep them from getting on the aircraft in the first place. As that security official observed, 'The key with airline security is a combination of good intelligence and physical security measures, with a heavy emphasis on passenger profiling.'"

SM: "Where have I heard that before?"

DB: "There was one aspect of that story that got my attention. The security official would prefer having former soldiers - with combat and special forces training—to become armed air marshals, but to wear civilian clothing on flights. '(They) would mingle with other passengers before they boarded the plane and look for signs of potential trouble throughout the flight.'"

SM: "What is your concern?"

DB: "If armed marshals are in civilian clothes, the question is whether they would be a better deterrent than if they were in uniform. If in civilian clothes, chances are they only could be carrying sidearms. There also is the issue of how passengers would feel if they saw uniform armed guards on their flight. Some research needs to be done on this. My memory may be faulty on this, but I thought the Israelis used uniformed soldiers on El Al flights. Then, there is yet another issue that is a lot more complicated."

SM: "And, what is that?"

DB: "Suppose an armed guard or two is assigned to a flight from Tel Aviv to New York. Is that guard an Israeli and a U.S. sky marshal? Suppose there is an attempted hijacking within the territorial limit of the United States. Are there legal ramifications if the Israeli guard swings into action? Conversely, suppose the attempted hijacking takes place right after takeoff, and the guard is a U.S. marshal. Does he or she have the legal right to interfere? Do the same issues arise if the flight is from New York to Tel Aviv? Could there be a combination of an Israeli guard and a U.S. sky marshal? There may well be international arrangements for such situations that we do not know about. International treaties are hard to come by as it is. As with the United Nations, there often is more heat than light.

International negotiations often end up with what I would describe as toothless agreements."

SM: "You had some observations in your other book about international involvement."

DB: "As I noted, ICAO adopted what became known as the *Tokyo Convention*. All it did was provide for the return of hijacked aircraft to the nation of origin. A year later, ICAO passed the *Hague Convention*. While it called for punishment or extradition of airplane hijackers, the choice was left up o the signers of the pact. That same year, ICAO drafted a *Montreal Convention* that proposed severe penalties for attacks in flight, as well as a treaty under which any nation that protected, did not prosecute, or did not extradite hijackers would face an international boycott. Both efforts fell flatter than a pancake. So, as I said, trying to get international agreement on aircraft hijacking is not an easy thing to accomplish."

SM: "As far as you can recall, was there any agreement on weapons that guards could use?"

DB: "If you remember my recounting that Fort Dix fiasco, there was special ammunition that would not penetrate the skin of the aircraft. But, as I recall, there was some question about whether that ammunition would affect the electrical system. It is important to note that the security consultant I mentioned was quoted as saying that 'firearms would be the very last resort.' To me, that is very good advice, as was his further comment that 'it was unrealistic to expect (armed guards) presence to mean there would be no more hijack attempts. Yes, it will be a deterrent to certain people, but of course there will always be someone who suddenly commits a crazed act during the flight.'"

SM: "It sounds as if international cooperation was lukewarm at best."

DB: "If so, it was not because the Task Force did not try. We worked with our Department of State, as well as with other diplomatic bodies. In June 1970, the Task Force invited 54 nations to attend a briefing of our work, including Dr. Dailey's profile. However, each nation did its own thing. But, as you can tell by 9/11, a lot still remains to be done about international cooperation."

CHAPTER TWENTY SEVEN -
WHAT NEEDS TO BE DONE

SM: "So, where do we go from here?"

DB: "The first step seems hopeless - that is, eradicating Mideast terrorism. Pandora's Box that released the evils of terrorism was not opened only on 9/11. The 9/11 Commission's Final Report lists Mideast terrorist acts after terrorist acts over decades. What bothers me is that we do not seem to have learned many lessons from those acts. It almost seems to we turned a blind eye and a deaf ear to such happenings until they occurred on U.S. soil. But, as pointed out before, Mideast terrorists bombed the World Trade Center in 1993! What more wake-up call did we need, especially at the FAA? Tepid warnings? That was a bureaucratic response, and the agency should accept full blame for that."

SM: "But, the FAA wasn't solely to blame. There were all those intelligence dysfunctions."

DB: "Despite those dysfunctions, I blame the FAA for not wondering whether the 1993 Mideast terrorist act against the World Trade Center could be translated into a Mideast terrorist act against U.S. aircraft. I don't think that should have taken a Mideast terrorism expert to at least consider that possibility. Again, as I have pointed out, our Task Force Final Report clearly warned about the possibility of **terrorist hijackings** against our airplanes. And, that is why I say one of the real mistakes of 9/11 can be traced to the disbanding of the Task Force in 1970."

SM: "Are you saying all we are doing is locking the barn door after the horse has been stolen, as the old saying goes?"

DB: "What I am saying I don't think we are using the right response. After the spate of bombings in the Middle East in late July 2005, we start using random searches. That, to me, is like a doctor prescribing an aspirin for a headache that closer scrutiny would have discovered to be a brain tumor."

SM: "Okay, get specific now. What should we be doing ?"

DB: "I would strongly suggest going back to the approach Dr. Reighard and the Task Force took. That is, develop statistics on the acts of Mideast terrorism - how they occurred, where they occurred, how they were accomplished, et cetera. I suggest the result of that research would conclude that potential Mideast terrorist hijackers are *a fraction of 1 percent of the flying public in the U.S.* Using Dr. Dailey's approach, a list of common characteristics needs to be developed into a profile for those few people. Next, as our traveling team did, those characteristics need to be tested for verification of so few people being involved. If that proves out, then that profile needs to be Step One, not the metal detector. Let's give Mideast terrorists credit for being deadly creative on how to develop 'weapons' to use on specific targets."

SM: "Well, it ought to be easy to spot Mideast terrorists trying to board a flight, shouldn't it?"

DB: "I think you are headed for 'racial' profiling. I doubt such terrorists would look and dress like Mideast people. From what I have read about the spate of bombings, some of the terrorists blended into the surrounding crowd. Remember, under Dr. Dailey's profile, a 'suspect' had to trigger at least half a dozen of the behavioral characteristics. Passenger screening has to be precise to be effective. In late July 2005, a flight was diverted because some passengers became suspicious of three 'Arab-looking' men walking up and down the aisles. It turned out that the three men were innocent businessmen. Had the adjusted profile been Step One, and the men were stopped before boarding, they would have been taken aside and questioned. If they had produced proper identification, and been subjected to a body search, they would have been cleared. The flight crew would have known about this, so that when other passengers because concerned, they could have been assured that the three men were 'kosher.'"

SM: "If I understand the point you are making in this case, that plane never would have been diverted."

DB: "That also goes back to what I said about the need to clear innocent passengers as quickly as possible. That approach was part of the Task Force effort to allay the fears of the major airlines that our search procedure would ruin their business. It is interesting that passenger traffic remains high even though they willingly put up with long security lines. What I am saying is that I don't think the overwhelming majority of air travelers should have to put up with those delays. But, we keep hearing and reading stories of those humiliating body searches."

SM: "Wouldn't we be taking a chance on clearing those passengers, some of whom may be Mideast terrorists in disguise?"

DB: "That was the same concern when our Task Force was in operation. To repeat, we felt there was no way to stop all hijacking attempts, even when most of them would end up in Cuba, and the hijackers were not terrorists. I don't care what system is in effect today - determined Mideast terrorists will give up their lives to accomplish their goal of hijacking an airplane if that is their plan. With all the military might we have in Iraq and Afghanistan, those terrorists still are giving us fits."

SM: "You've spent more time telling me what has gone wrong than what has gone right So, let's get specific on what you feel should be done to stop making screening, as you describe it 'ineffective, inefficient, and humiliating.'"

DB: "Fair enough. **First**, I would ask top decision makers to read the Task Force Final Report, which is FAA Manual AM-78-35, especially the pages I enumerated that contain those dire predictions three decades before they actually happened."

SM: "As I recall, the Manual is available from the National Technical Information Service."

DB: "**Second,** I would ask decision makers to study how Dr. Dailey created his profile through data analysis, how we tested it, why the ACLU approved it, and how a New York Federal Court judge ruled the procedure constitutional. So, I am asking decision makers to use the same epidemiological approach Dr. Dailey did to reach *realistic* conclusions instead of *political* ones. As such, I ask decision makers to adapt Dr. Dailey's profile to present-day circumstances, but to insure such profile be Step One. That would enable *innocent* passengers to be quickly cleared and boarded."

SM: "What would come next?"

DB: "**Third,** I would ask decision makers to understand that this approach not only can save millions and millions of dollars badly needed for domestic programs, but also to making screening *more efficient, more effective, and less humiliating.* That can be done by having one set of screening procedures for *potential Mideast terrorist hijackers* but another set for *potential non-Mideast terrorist hijackers* such as 'disturbed' domestic offenders."

SM: "That's something I have not heard before. Go on, please."

DB: "**Fourth,** I would ask decision makers to work more closely with airline officials to expedite baggage inspections so that the flow to and from aircraft is as smooth and fast as possible within bounds of security. That may include another look at carry-on luggage. During our testing, we worked closely with Eastern Airlines first, and others later, to hear what they had to say. We did not want to put a crimp on airline passenger revenue."

SM: "I am led to believe this is being done, but I understand your concern about trying to improve whatever is being done."

DB: "**Fifth,** I would ask decision makers to develop a positive rapport with the news media. We worked hard at that, often asking trusted reporters how they would treat our efforts. We also tried to anticipate reporters' questions and concerns. We did not want to read, hear, and see stories about how messed up the system was. That is why we were so adamant about testing our procedure not only to determine the effect it would have on passengers, but also to get a feel for how reporters would treat our efforts."

SM: "Are you saying you wanted to control the media?"

DB: "Absolutely not! On the contrary, we wanted to be as open as we could with the media without bounds of security. As I already have explained, we emphasized why we had bounds of security. Of course, the media today are not the media of yesterday. That is why there has to be a new way of dealing with the media. As a former reporter, I role-played with my colleagues to get their reaction. Naturally, there will be those reporters who for whatever motive will not find anything positive to say. And, if you recall, out of some 200 stories I documented during our testing phase when we had news conferences at every airport we used, only half a dozen were negative. You just have to accept that, and as the old Johnny Mercer tune goes, 'Accentuate the positive.'"

SM: I hope you do not plan to sing that song."

DB: "You really do not want to hear me try to sing. **Sixth,** I would hope decision makers would read other books on earlier events, such as Jim Arey's *The Skyjackers.*"

SM: "You're asking a lot, especially relating this to current terrorism activities."

DB: "Well, look how security officials still are trying to come to grips with screening methods. The Associated Press reported in mid-April 2005 that according to 'a House member who has been briefed on the contents' that '(t)wo upcoming government reports will say the quality of screening at airports is no better now than before the Sept. 11 attacks.'"

SM: "Any more suggestions?"

DB: "One last one. **Seventh,** I hope decision makers develop an apolitical understanding not only of what motivates Mideast terrorists, but also how any Mideast terrorist hijacking provides a floor plan of how we can create and test the proper procedures to deal with that. Assuming that all domestic passengers are *potential Mideast terrorist hijackers is* the *wrong approach.*"

SM: "What makes you think you have the answers?"

DB: "I'm not offended by that question at all. Neither Dr. Dailey nor I pretend to have all the answers. What we are saying is that present day procedures do not have a sound basis or premise. It almost is like tossing darts at a procedure board in front of you, and wherever they land, that is the procedure *de jour*. Random searches in this scheme of things are unrealistic because they are. nothing more than knee-jerk reactions just for the sake of reactions. The very nature of uncertainty prevails today. What amazes me is that passengers are willing to put up with delays and humiliation because why consider political brainwashing when there are more efficient, effective, and less humiliating ways to accomplish security."

SM: "Is there anything we have not covered that you would like to bring up?"

DB: "If you can spare the time, you might be interested in the relationship between Dr. Dailey's profile and my endless battle with The New York Times on who deserves the credit for the only psychological profile used to screen passengers."

SM: "You've got my attention on that one."

CHAPTER TWENTY EIGHT -
THESE ARE THE (NEW YORK) TIMES THAT
TRY A MAN'S PROFESSIONAL SOUL

DB: "On January 16, 2005, The Times Sunday Magazine ran an article titled *The First Hijackers - Re-Evaluation* by Andreas Killen. The article did not identify the author, nor present any credentials to justify writing such an article. In recounting a number of pre-9/11 hijackers, Killen cited 'an influential study, *The Skyjacker*, by David Hubbard (who) enumerated common passengers' responses to hijackings. Hubbard, a psychiatrist, was hired by the F.A.A. to create the psychological profile used for screening passengers."

SM: "Just a minute. All along you have been telling me that it was Dr. Dailey who did that."

DB: "Of course. The minute I saw those words, I fired off an e-mail letter-to-the-editor. I challenged the allegation that Hubbard had some such a profile, since I was on the Task Force from beginning to end. I cited the Manual and my own previous book, *NINE/ELEVEN*, which detailed the work of our group to show that only Dr. Dailey's profile was *the* (meaning only) profile 'used for screening passengers." I also cited the ACLU approval and the New York Federal Court case. About a week later, I received a call from a Sarah H. Smith, a fact checker. In essence, she said her staff had 'evidence' to support the reference to Hubbard. By the way, I said I found it interesting that (1) the article did not properly refer to him as Dr.

Hubbard - a psychiatrist being a medical doctor, and (2) questioning **why a psychiatrist** would produce a **psychological profile.** She would not back down. On January 25, I e-mailed her stating that I checked with a former FAA colleague who did some later work for the Task Force, and he said he never heard of Dr. Hubbard. Checking with Dr. Dailey, he agreed that Dr. Hubbard was one of some 200 people who submitted ideas to deal with the then hijackings, mostly to Cuba."

SM: "What was his suggestion?"

DB: "As John and I best recall, he wanted prostitutes put aboard flights to entice hijackers because he felt hijackers had sexual problems."

SM: "You're putting me on."

DB: "In all honesty, that is our recollection. Anyhow, I followed that e-mail up the next day wanting to see her 'evidence.' I said I had searched the Internet and could not find any reference to Dr. Hubbard except that he wrote that book. I suggested she read the Task Force Final Report as well as the New York Federal Court decision where John's profile was specifically cited. I also noted that the FAA gave John its highest cash award at the time, $3,000, for his profile work. Two days later, I sent her another e-mail stating that I just bought Dr. Hubbard's book, and read it carefully from front to back. I stated, 'NOWHERE IN ALL 262 PAGES WILL YOU FIND ONE MENTION - JUST ONE MENTION - OF ANYTHING TO BACK UP WHAT YOU BELIEVE IS THE FACT THAT HE WAS HIRED BY THE FAA TO CREATE A PSYCHOLOGICAL PROFILE USED FOR PASSENGER SCREENING.' I'd like to talk more about his book later. I mentioned that during my reporter days, I handled letters to the editor."

SM: "That must have gotten her attention."

DB: "Indeed it did. On February 8, she e-mailed me with this long one-paragraph response: 'I was surprised to get your letter of 2/6/05. (I have not recounted every e-mail I sent, but she cited eight of them.) It takes time to determine whether a correction is warranted in a case like this, where there seems to be evidence supporting both sides.. I am grateful for our continuing patience and hope that you will understand that I have not dismissed your concerns, but am addressing them with the same care with which I respond to all our correspondents.'"

SM: "Sounds reasonable to me."

DB: "I suppose I should have been flattered by being called a correspondent. Anyhow, she also said she never received a copy of my book that I had sent. So, I mailed a second one with a return card. She never acknowledged receiving it, but the Post Office assured me it got to The Times. Be that as it may, I sent another e-mail that same day saying that 'I would appreciate a look at what you describe as evidence supporting the claim that Dr. Hubbard was the one hired by the FAA to develop a psychological profile used to screen passengers.' I also stated I had surfed Google looking for such evidence, but could not find any. I added that 'this issue has gone on for a month. For the final time, I ask that you let me know exactly what evidence you and/or your staff have found to support Dr. Hubbard's claim.'"

SM: "You seem to be getting nowhere slowly."

DB: I do not give up easily. On February 20, I sent yet another e-mail arguing, 'I cannot fathom why you deign to protect the article's author when you cannot provide me with supporting material.' I sent copies to The Times Executive Editor Bill Keller and to Public Editor (the ombudsman) Dan Okrent."

SM: "That should have gotten someone's attention."

DB: "Yes."

SM: " Well, finally.'"

DB: "An aide to the Public Editor e-mailed me saying he could not find any 'record of any correspondence between you and this office going back three months. Please forward any previous correspondence between us so that I may raise the issue with the appropriate editors.' I responded with a long e-mail recounting the correspondence. The following day, the Public Editor himself e-mailed me saying, 'I haven't dropped this yet. I should be able to get back to you with something definitive in a matter of days."

SM: "Hope springs eternal."

DB: "I was naive to hope so. But, I did find it odd that on the previous day, his aide said he could not find any correspondence from me, but within 24 hours his boss clearly intimated that he had been looking into the matter. The Public Editor sent another e-mail later that day stating, 'I have begun to look into your concern. We usually tell readers that this process may take up to two weeks. We will certainly try to expedite this but I cannot guarantee you of an immediate response.' He also said I should send e-mails directly to him because copies are not considered. To me, an e-mail is an e-mail whether it is sent directly, or is a copy. The following day, the aide got back into the act stating, 'We ask readers not to cc. us on this they want us to respond to because we get spammed and needlessly cc'd on letters which have nothing to do with this office and while we review these messages the volume of messages we receive force us to focus our full attention on messages sent directly to us.'"

SM: "Well, that cleared things up."

DB: "You josh. On March 16, I noted that the following day 'marks two months since I challenged this story.' And still no answers to my challenges. So much for rapid response. I sent yet another e-mail reminder on March 30, which did prompt a response from the Public Editor. He stated, 'I have advised the editors of the magazine that it would appear to be inaccurate to say that Dr. Hubbard was commissioned to do a profile.'"

SM: "Your patience was finally rewarded."

DB: "Not so fast. The next sentence noted that 'a correction might be phrased to indicate that he was not commissioned to do the profile, but was one of several consulted on the subject.'"

SM: "I'm not sure what to make of that."

DB: "What I made of it was a typical bureaucratic 'spin.' I worked in the government for 24 years, and I know a 'spin' when I see one. Of course, now I really wanted the evidence to prove Dr. Hubbard even was a consultant But, the Public Editor beat me to the punch."

SM: "I think I need an aspirin at this point."

DB: "He went on to say, 'However, they (the editors) point out that they have no independent proof that he was not commissioned to do a profile, and that a correction without such proof might in turn be inaccurate.'"

SM: "Come again?"

DB: "On the one hand, he admitted there was no proof that Dr. Hubbard did what the article claimed he did, but on the other, there was no proof that Dr. Hubbard was not hired to do it. The Public Editor continued, 'Given how far in the past these events took place such proof may not be available. However, if you could provide authoritative assertion from someone without a vested interest in discrediting Dr. Hubbard, I would of course become more insistent about a correction. I'm not suggesting that you aren't being truthful with me - only that you yourself may not have access to all the available information.'"

SM: "What was your response to that?"

DB: "If I were a Times fact-checker, I would have contacted the FAA. If Dr. Hubbard had been hired as a consultant, there had to be some record of his work, if nothing else to justify whatever money he would have been paid. But, I resisted the urge to insult The Times by telling the paper how to do some solid and basic investigating."

SM: "Was that the end of it?"

DB: "Not by a long shot. The Public Editor e-mailed me wanting me to ask Dr. Dailey to tell him what Dr. Hubbard's role was. First of all, I gave Okrent John's phone number, feeling it was up to him to make the call, not get me involved as a third party. Second, I already had e-mailed The Tunes what John had confirmed with me. What more could I do? So, once again, I asked to see the so-called 'evidence' that Dr. Hubbard did what the article claimed he had done."

SM: "What did Dr. Dailey say?"

DB: "I called John several days later. He said he never received the call. But then, I saw an article in The Times that Okrent was ending his contract as Public Editor at the end of April, and that Byron Calame would replace him. But, I had one more go with Okrent. On April 21, I e-mailed him noting that a Los Angeles Times reporter was fired for not being able to verify the courses of some quotations he used. I compared that lack of verification with the case here. As you phrased it early, I got nowhere slowly. That means, no response from Okrent."

SM: "Why didn't you just give up at this point?"

DB: "No me. I then wrote a letter on May 5 to Times Publisher Arthur Ochs Sulzberger, Jr., recounting my frustration."

SM: "Did he respond?"

DB: "The response came from Allan M. Siegel, assistant managing editor and the 'standards editor' of The Times. I never knew such a title existed. In a May 11 letter, Siegel sent me a copy of the correction that appeared in the May 8 issue of the Sunday Magazine. I had missed it."

SM: "You finally won the battle, to my surprise."

DB: "If only that were true."

SM: "Run that by me again?"

DB: "The correction read: 'An article on Jan. 16, about aircraft hijackings in the 1970's, referred imprecisely to the role played by a psychiatrist, Dr. **David Hubbard** (yes, bold letters), in the creation of a psychological profile of potential hijackers for the F.A.A. Dr. Hubbard did develop such a profile, used by both the government and industry. But an F.A.A. task force in operation from 1969 to 1971 developed an earlier profile of potential hijackers, relying on the work of one of its members, John T. Dailey. This omission was brought to the attention of the editors shortly after the article appeared, and this correction was delayed for further research.'"

SM: "So, that ended the matter."

DB: "Hardly. First of all, Dr. Hubbard, a psychiatrist, would not be doing a psychological profile. The two professions may have some common ground, but a psychiatrist has to be a medical doctor; a psychologist does not. Second, the correction reiterated that Dr. Hubbard 'did develop such a profile,' still without providing any proof. Third, the Task Force ended its work in 1970, not 1971. That is sloppy journalism. Fourth, while the correction did use the title Dr. for Hubbard, it did not do the same for Dailey, who has a doctorate. That too is sloppy journalism. And, fifth, the correction kept referring to 'potential' hijackers. They all were actual hijackers. Even sloppier journalism. But, the kicker was Siegel's accompanying letter."

SM: "What did it say?"

DB: "One sentence tells it all: 'Quite honestly I cannot imagine what further research would have taken us nearly four months to carry out, but I hope all's well that ends well.'"

SM: "What do I get the feeling that this did not end things well?"

DB: "A new chapter was about to unfold. I suddenly received a phone call from someone who only identified himself as Bill Borders of The Times. He said he was conducting an impartial inquiry into the matter. We went over the entire matter, and he said he would call back. When he did, he said he concluded The Times did all it could, and nothing more could be done."

SM: "Another anticlimax? What more could be done?"

DB: "I e-mailed Borders, who never told me what position he held, offering the following proposed correction: 'A May 8 correction referring to a January 16 New York Times Sunday Magazine article about aircraft hijackings needs further clarification. While the article stated that Dr. David Hubbard, a psychiatrist, 'created the psychological profile used for screening passengers,' further research has concluded that the only (such) profile was created by Dr. John T. Dailey, a member of the agency's Task Force on Deterrence of Air Piracy and the FAA's chief psychologist. His profile was tested during 1969-70. While Dr. Hubbard in his book *The Skyjacker* established a psychiatric profile of hijackers, there is no evidence that he was hired by the FAA to apply his conclusions to a passenger screening procedure.'"

SM: "And, when did that appear?"

DB: "You jest. Nothing ever appeared."

SM: "What was your next move?"

DB: "I e-mailed the new Public Editor. On June 8, he responded: 'I consider the Dailey-Hubbard dispute over credit for profiling a question that has been dealt with appropriately by Allan M. Siegel. I have plenty to do in dealing with new issues, so I don't envision revisiting the Dailey-Hubbard question.'"

SM: "I guess that put you in your place."

DB: "Pretty much. I tried several more times to plead my case, but Siegel ended it all in a July 5 letter: 'I don't know what else we can do to satisfy you that The Times has considered your position repeatedly and as objectively as we know how. I sent out your position fully in a letter to you on June 16, which also cited earlier conversations between you and William Borders. I am sorry that I cannot think of any further recourse we can properly accord you.'"

SM: "End of your journalistic journey."

DB: "Yes, from that perspective. But, then comes a piece by Op-Ed Editor David Shipley in the July 31 Times. The subtitle is ironic: 'When you're working with other people's words, there are clear rules of engagement.'"

SM: "I don't get the irony."

DB: "Apparently, what's good for the Op-Ed page is not good for the Sunday Magazine."

SM: "You need to clarify that for me."

DB: "Here is what the Op-Ed editor said his staff will do with submissions: 'Correct grammatical and typographical errors. Make sure that the article conforms to The New York Times Manual of Style and Usage. See to it that the article fits our allotted space. Fact-check the article.'"

SM: "Now I see where you are going with this."

DB: "Just for a moment, let's see what the Op-Ed editor says about fact-checking: 'While it is the author's responsibility to ensure that everything written for us is accurate, we still check facts - names, dates, places, quotations. We also check assertions. If news articles - from The Times or other publications - are at odds with a point or an example in an essay, we need to resolve whatever discrepancy exists.... we'd discuss it with the writer ... and we'd try to find a solution that preserves the writer's argument while also adhering to the facts."

SM: "So, if I understand the point you are making is that it was up to the Magazine editors to have the writer of that January 16 article verify the assertion about Dr. Hubbard having developed a profile similar to Dr. Dailey's."

DB: "Since Dr. Dailey's profile was a psychological one, all I asked for was the so-called 'evidence' that Dr. Hubbard created a psychological profile. The May 8 correction cleverly avoided that."

SM: "Okay. Let's go on to Dr. Hubbard's book."

CHAPTER TWENTY NINE -
THE HUBBARD HUBBUB

DB: "Dr. Hubbard undertook a psychiatric look at hijacking in his 1971 book. The inside cover is quite revealing: 'Virtually all of those interviewed proved to be effeminate, sexually inadequate, ineffectual, generally apolitical individuals who have skyjacked in situations of total personal failure as a decisive act to get themselves killed or at least out of this world. The offenders themselves tended to be sexually confused, weak moma's boys.' Dr. Hubbard also contended that hijackers were influenced by the force of gravity."

SM: "I must admit this seems to support your argument that he looked at skyjackers strictly from a psychiatric point of view."

DB: "He had some other interesting observations. On Pages 230 and 231, he proposed an international agreement for *'the immediate return of all offenders for hospitalization, study and disposition.'* He concluded that this agreement 'would put a stop to the crime in short order.' He also stressed research on the relationship between skyjackers and 'sexual inadequacy.'"

SM: "He certainly seems fixated on the sexuality of skyjackers."

DB: "I found a web site that noted Dr. Hubbard testified for the defense in a case involving a skyjacker identified only as 'Greg Ross.' Dr. Hubbard asserted that the defendant 'was schizophrenic, that he deserved to be treated not as a criminal but as a sick man and that hijackers often suffer from a sense of masculine failure and latent homosexuality.' Having said all of that, there is nothing in his book that shows how his psychiatric conclusions could be translated into a psychological screening of passengers."

SM: "By the way, what do you think of the Transportation Security Administration?"

CHAPTER THIRTY - TSK, TSK, TSA

DB: "Having had my say, in the final analysis, I almost feel sorry for the TSA."

SM: "What do you mean by that?"

DB: "First, it had to absorb the FAA's Office of Civil Aviation Security, with its benign attitude about Mideast terrorists and potential hijacking of U.S. aircraft although we warned about that possibility as far back as 1978. Second, it had to try to implement sometimes conflicting procedures to screen passengers. As if those CAPPS systems weren't enough-of a headache, they were preceded by TIPs - Threat Image Protection-to check baggage for weapons. And, I don't even want to get into those Color Card warnings. But, in June 2005, The Washington Post reported, 'A new air-security system designed to track foreign visitors arriving in the United States has mistakenly snagged dozens of crew members of foreign airlines, according to new documents obtained from the Department of Homeland Security.' And, DHS is the boss of TSA. Having worked in government for nearly a quarter of a century, I know that political appointees dictate the programs that civil servants are forced to implement without question. Homeland Security Secretary Michael Chertoff had to face the wrath of members of a House Appropriations Subcommittee in March 2005 to defend the agency's budget. One subcommittee member called the agency 'dysfunctional.' Barely a month later, The Washington Post reported that TSA chief David

M. Stone was resigning, citing 'budget constraints and changes in leadership.' The ranking Democrat on the agency's oversight committee, Congressman Peter A. DeFazio of California, was cited as fearing 'Stone's departure signals a push by Republicans to dismantle the TSA and replace federal airport screeners, with ones employed by private companies.'"

SM: "Doesn't sound promising."

DB: "As if that were not enough, The Post followed up that story with one noting that 'Stone is the third top administrator to leave the three-year-old agency. The TSA has been plagued by operational missteps, public relations blunders and criticism of its performance from the public and legislators.' It gets even better. 'Its (No Fly) list has mistakenly snared senators. Its security screeners have been arrested for stealing from luggage, and its passenger pat-downs have set off an outcry from women.'"

SM: "And, you feel sorry for both DHS and TSA?"

DB: "I feel sorry for those who want to do a good job, but are like the proverbial lemmings marching down to the sea behind the Pied Piper of Hamelin. They just don't have a choice because chief decision makers are trying to address a criminal problem with a political solution."

SM: "Well, on that note, I want to thank you for sharing your thoughts with me, and for being so candid. Good luck on your book."

DB: "And, good luck on the hearings."

CHAPTER THIRTY ONE - FINAL THOUGHTS

There will be those who read this far and say, "Been there, done that," regarding airline screening and its relationship to terrorism in general.

The point of this book is to plead for a sound process in creating the most effective, efficient, and least intrusive screening system. Too many cooks are stirring the bureaucratic cauldron of terrorism, each one determining the right taste.

I reiterate that our Task Force was successful because it "thought outside the bureaucratic box." Our group played devil's advocate with one another every step of the way. We tried to anticipate what effect our procedure would have on potential hijackers, the public, and the media. We were staunchly apolitical.

What seems to be escaping those with whom I have discussed this book is the fact that our work enabled us to predict, literally and figuratively, what was to happen on 9/11. It was just a logical extension of our work. We also readily agreed that no one effort would stem the tide of hijacking, only deter it to a manageable number. What law enforcement official will assert that crime can be eliminated?

Terrorist airplane hijackings have been around for a long time. The twain does meet.

We took great pains to look at every possibility, even among the some 200 ideas submitted to us, no matter how ludicrous they seemed to be. We did not want to be accused of bureaucratically dismissing or overlooking anything using the excuse, "That's not the way it's been done before."

As to The New York Times, I remain professionally offended on two counts. One, the paper has stained the singular accomplishment of my friend and colleague, Dr. John T. Dailey. Two, The Times remains guilty of sloppy and hypocritical journalism.

EPILOGUE

Not one word of what was said here ever appeared in the 9/11 Commission's Final Report.

Neither of my two unique books on airline passenger screening and Mideast terrorism ever will make it to The New York Times Best Seller List.

The Times never revealed its Sunday Magazine article's "anonymous source" to justify its continuing assertion that a **psychiatrist** created a second **psychological** study like the one developed by Dr. John T. Dailey. In an August 28, 2005 Public Editor column in The Times, the aforementioned Mr. Siegel was quoted as saying that "if it isn't obvious from the story why we permitted the material to be used anonymously, what was the rationale? What were the attempts to go back to the source?" The Times may be guilty of hypocrisy in my case.

On August 13, 2005, The Washington Post reported on Page 1 that Edmund S. Hawley, administrator of the Transportation Security Administration, "directed his staff to propose changes in how the agency screens 2 million passengers a day." Not only will the ban on various carry-on items be lifted, but "passengers no longer (will) routinely be required to remove their shoes at security checkpoint," the article noted. The headline read: "Airline Security Changes Planned." The sub-headline was: "Threats Reassessed to Make Travel Easier for Public." Read my tips, Administrator Hawley.

On August 30, 2005, the "On the Road" column in The New York Times quoted former Secretary of Homeland Security Tom Ridge as admitting, "I have been pulled into secondary inspection about a dozen times since I became a private citizen." It also cited Ridge as saying, "We need to move from looking for weapons to paying attention to people who are or could be terrorists."

Printed in the United States
93317LV00008B/6/A